SAP R/3 Enterprise Software

An Introduction

SAP R/3 Enterprise Software

An Introduction

Roger Hayen

Boston   Burr Ridge, IL   Dubuque, IA   Madison, WI   New York   San Francisco   St. Louis
Bangkok   Bogotá   Caracas   Kuala Lumpur   Lisbon   London   Madrid   Mexico City
Milan   Montreal   New Delhi   Santiago   Seoul   Singapore   Sydney   Taipei   Toronto

SAP R/3 ENTERPRISE SOFTWARE: AN INTRODUCTION
Published by McGraw-Hill/Irwin, a business unit of The McGraw-Hill Companies, Inc., 1221 Avenue
of the Americas, New York, NY, 10020. Copyright © 2007 by The McGraw-Hill Companies, Inc. All
rights reserved. No part of this publication may be reproduced or distributed in any form or by any
means, or stored in a database or retrieval system, without the prior written consent of The McGraw-Hill
Companies, Inc., including, but not limited to, in any network or other electronic storage or transmission,
or broadcast for distance learning.

Some ancillaries, including electronic and print components, may not be available to customers outside
the United States.

This book is printed on acid-free paper.

1 2 3 4 5 6 7 8 9 0 QPD/QPD 0 9 8 7 6

ISBN-13: 978-0-07-299067-6
ISBN-10: 0-07-299067-8

Editorial director: *Stewart Mattson*
Executive editor: *Richard T. Hercher, Jr.*
Editorial assistant: *Katie Jones*
Executive marketing manager: *Rhonda Seelinger*
Media producer: *Greg Bates*
Project manager: *Jim Labeots*
Lead production supervisor: *Rose Hepburn*
Designer: *Jillian Lindner*
Lead media project manager: *Brian Nacik*
Cover design: *Jillian Lindner*
Cover image: *Cover photograph by Stephen Codrington*
Typeface: *10/12 Palatino*
Compositor: *Interactive Composition Corporation*
Printer: *Quebecor World Dubuque Inc.*

Library of Congress Cataloging-in-Publication Data

Hayen, Roger L.
    SAP R/3 enterprise software : an introduction / Roger Hayen.
        p. cm.
    Includes index.
    ISBN-13: 978-0-07-299067-6 (alk. paper)
    ISBN-10: 0-07-299067-8 (alk. paper)
        1. SAP R/3. 2. Business—Data processing. 3. Management information systems.
I. Title.
HF5548.4.R2H39 2007
650.0285'53769—dc22

                                                                                    2006041959

www.mhhe.com

To Dakota Marie, our newest family member and a shining light in our lives, who has yet to learn the letters S A P, but whose life will be touched in many ways by information technology.

—Hayen

About the Author

Roger Hayen

Roger Hayen is the Towle Professor of Management Information Systems in the Department of Business Information Systems of the College of Business Administration at Central Michigan University. Since 1997, he has continued to work on integrating the SAP R/3 Enterprise Software into the college's curriculum. During this time, he has developed and taught courses that include an introduction to SAP R/3 software, ABAP programming, and SAP R/3 configuration and implementation. His current curriculum development efforts include integrating the SAP R/3 software into the Information Systems course and other courses required of all majors in the College of Business Administration. He has published several articles that describe various efforts in integrating SAP R/3 software in college and university curricula.

Brief Table of Contents

Table of Contents

Preface

This book explores enterprise software by using the SAP R/3 Enterprise System as its example software. The purpose of the book is to provide you with a good, overall understanding of enterprise software including what it is, how it is used, and how it is deployed in business organizations.

SAP R/3 Enterprise software encompasses most of the common business applications that organizations use to manage their day-to-day business activities—general ledger, purchasing, order entry, accounts receivable, accounts payable, payroll, and inventory. This book introduces the deployment of the SAP R/3 Enterprise software in business organizations. We relate R/3 Enterprise (formerly known as SAP R/3 System) to an information systems framework, examine its technical structure, and consider general implementation issues. Key issues explored concentrate on the features involved with the deployment of enterprise software in achieving organizational objectives. Implementation issues include configuring R/3 Enterprise to meet specific business workflow requirements and managing the implementation project. We examine the role of Solution Manager with the Accelerated SAP methodology by carrying out and managing implementation activities. Understanding the concepts and issues of R/3 Enterprise will give you an overall understanding of the use of enterprise software. You should gain a fundamental understanding of the R/3 Enterprise software and its use in organizations. You should be ready to begin to learn the details of working with the individual modules of the R/3 Enterprise software after you have examined these topics: Overview, Application Modules, Business Processes, Navigation and Systems Operation, Web Application Server, Internet-Enabled Solutions, Configuration, Implementation Framework, Implementation Planning, Organization Structure, and Customizing Tools.

The book is arranged in three parts with the following general content:

PART ONE—Understanding Enterprise Software

This is an introduction to the concepts of enterprise software and its deployment in organizations. It provides a conceptual foundation of enterprise software and the business supply chain. The application modules that support supply chain management are introduced and examined. The use of the Accelerated SAP methodology in deploying the R/3 Enterprise System in an organization is considered.

PART TWO—Displaying SAP R/3 Information

This is an introduction to the hands-on navigation and operation of the R/3 System using the IDES training data for Version 4.7. Typical R/3 System transaction screens are displayed to familiarize you with the navigation and structure of R/3 Enterprise transactions.

PART THREE—Processing SAP R/3 Transactions

This is a more in-depth, hands-on exploration of the R/3 System using the IDES training data for Version 4.7. You create data for the processing of typical transactions. This builds upon the navigation skill from Part 2 while exploring many of the fundamental transactions that support supply chain management processing throughout the customer order to cash cycle.

You should complete the Overview and Navigation and Systems Operation in Part 1 before doing Part 2. Additionally, you should complete Application Modules and Business Processes in Part 1 together with Part 2 before doing Part 3. These combinations of the three parts of the book allow you to integrate the hands-on, step-by-step R/3 System processing activities with your study of the underlying concepts of the R/3 Enterprise System.

When you have completed all three parts of the book, you should have a very good understanding of what the SAP R/3 Enterprise System and enterprise software are. You should be ready to begin working with the R/3 System in a business organization and have the introductory knowledge needed to begin more advanced study of the system and enterprise software.

Acknowledgments

I would like to thank the many people who contributed to the successful completion of *SAP Enterprise Software: An Introduction.*

I am grateful to SAP AG for encouraging my university to be the fifth one joining their University Alliance Program, which made their software available to us for teaching and research. This alliance has made this book possible and continues to integrate enterprise system technology in education.

I would like to thank the many people at McGraw-Hill/Irwin for their efforts in completing this project: Dick Hercher, Katie Jones, Jim Labeots, and Pat Forrest at Carlisle Publishers Services.

I am grateful for the many suggestions and valuable insights provided by my colleagues. The faculty and staff in the Business Information Systems Department at Central Michigan University encouraged and supported the book's formulation and development in a variety of ways. The department chair, Monica Holmes, provided considerable direction and encouragement in completing this book.

I would also like to thank the following reviewers for their excellent work: Ray Boykin, Cal State—Chico; Shad Dowlatshahi, University of Missouri—Kansas City; Seong-Jong Joo, Central Washington University; Alden Lorents, Northern Arizona University; Sundar Srinivasan, University of Missouri—Rolla; Lou Thompson, University of Texas—Dallas; and Vincent Yu, University of Missouri—Rolla.

And last but not least, I would like to thank my wife, Sandy. During this project, the book overshadowed many family activities and produced many late nights, but her encouragement, support, and most of all, perseverance, enabled me to complete this project.

Roger Hayen

Understanding Enterprise Software

Part 1

Chapter 1

Overview

What Is Enterprise Software?

Enterprise software is integrated software that facilitates the flow of information among all the main processes of a business: from sales order entry to manufacturing to invoicing to collection. It is comprehensive, packaged software that joins together the complete range of business processes and functions. Enterprise software provides a holistic view of business within a single information systems (IS) technology architecture. These systems exhibit broad but tightly integrated functionality. They encompass the core transaction-processing activities of a business enterprise—that is, all the processes of an organization's supply chain. A **supply chain** describes the chronological and logical relationships of business transactions from raw material supplies to finished goods and final consumption. Those activities in the supply chain that add value to a product or service of an organization are its **value chain.** A value chain encompasses all the business events from the receipt of a customer order to the delivery of that order. For example, value is added when the production processes take raw materials and transform them into a finished product, and when that product is sold to a customer. A company is profitable if the price consumers are willing to pay for a product exceeds the costs of creating value.

For example, with integrated software, Brenda in the sales and marketing department can check on the quantity of a product that is available for shipment to a customer while she is on the phone. She can tell the customer how much is available and where it is, regardless of whether the location is down the street or halfway around the world. Before Brenda completes her conversation with the customer, the order can be confirmed, the credit check approved, and shipment of the order to the customer initiated from the closest location. If there is inadequate product in inventory, the production of any additional quantity can be scheduled and an expected delivery date set. All this is done within one integrated business software application. Without integrated software, Brenda would need to access several different systems to check on the quantity in inventory, the customer's available credit, the production schedule, and the shipping schedule. What she was able to accomplish in a matter of minutes while on the phone with her customer would likely take several days without an integrated system.

What Is ERP?

Enterprise resource planning (ERP) is frequently viewed as the software that supports its related business functionality. That is, **ERP software** is yesterday's term for today's enterprise software (ES), which has evolved beyond the earlier capabilities associated with ERP software. Clearly, ES is more than just resource planning for an enterprise. You can gain a better understanding of ERP software by considering the manner in which this software grew with advances in computing power.

In the 1960s many software packages used by business included an inventory control (IC) capability. The ongoing development of this software guided the creation of a next generation of **material requirements planning** (MRP) systems during the 1970s. These MRP systems used a master production schedule and a bill of materials that contained a list of materials needed to manufacture each product. Hence, they served a major role in planning a company's production. As they continued to evolve (see **Figure 1.1**), MRP systems were enhanced by adding features for sales planning, customer order processing, and rough-cut capacity planning. These enhancements provided a closed-loop MRP system, which furnished input into production scheduling that is a planning process. The ongoing development of this software resulted in MRPII ("MRP-two") systems in the 1980s that incorporated even more functional features of financial accounting and of other manufacturing and materials management systems. These systems continued to be developed in parallel with computing capabilities and resulted in better integration of material and capacity requirements for production that were translated into financial information. They became much more than just their initial focus on inventory control and material requirements.

By the 1990s, these earlier systems had evolved even further to provide seamless integration of all information flows in a company, including financial accounting, human resource management, supply chain management, and customer information. They became known as **ERP systems.** However, the evolution of these systems continued, again aided by increased computing power at ever decreasing costs. More features and better integration were added to the software to support the entire value chain of business operations, that is, the **order-to-cash cycle,** from the receipt of a customer order until the cash payment was received from the customer for that order. With all these enhanced features, ERP and ERP software became far more than what was implied by the word "planning" in "enterprise resource planning"—a better, more descriptive name was needed. Enterprise software of the 2000s is the result of this continuing evolution. ES not only encapsulates the functionality of ERP software and its predecessors, but it also provides better integration and more functionality that meets information processing needs for an entire business enterprise. What does the future hold for the next generation, the 2010s? Surely a new name will be needed by then. The ES integration presented in this book includes the functionality of what has come before in ERP software and represents the next generation in integrated business-processing software. This book is about the next wave of ERP software—enterprise

FIGURE 1.1
Timeline of Integrated Software Generation Developments

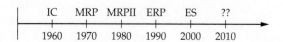

software—exemplified by the most popular software product of this type: SAP R/3. In some manner, enterprise software will touch your life in the future. Whether you are traveling on Delta Airlines, making a purchase at Home Depot, or working for a company such as Dow Chemical, enterprise software will be at the heart of how business transactions will be conducted.

What Is SAP R/3?

SAP R/3 is enterprise software because it is integrated and encompasses the primary aspects of supply chain processing. That is, R/3 Enterprise is information systems technology for the core business processing that supports **supply chain management** (SCM). R/3 Enterprise provides information for managing supply chain activities. R/3 Enterprise consists of a series of integrated core business application modules for transaction processing. These modules contain a set of functions that implement best business practices for SCM activities. A **best business practice** is a ready-made business process, such as customer order entry, that reflects the combined experiences, suggestions, and requirements of leading companies in a host of industries.

R/3 Enterprise is more than software modules that implement best business practices. It contains integrated tools that make it possible to implement very different organization structures and processing requirements. That is, the tools to customize an R/3 Enterprise system to meet an organization's specific requirements are built into the software. They are not a separate add-on that is used only for customization. So, both the business processes and the customization tools are integrated into the R/3 Enterprise system. Fundamentally, everything you need to run a business is included in the best business practice processes, while everything you need to set up the R/3 Enterprise system to meet your specific organizational requirements is also included.

Who Is SAP?

SAP (Systems, Applications, and Products in Data Processing) AG was founded in 1972 in Walldorf, Germany. It is the world's leading business application software company. In 1992, SAP launched its R/3 System, which runs in a client/server environment. This product has seen phenomenal growth. From a zero base in 1992 until 2002, over 17,500 organizations had installations, an average annual growth rate of 166 percent. These organizations represent an estimated 10 million users served by the R/3 System. SAP markets its products all over the world to almost every industry as well as to government, educational institutions, and hospitals.

Application Modules

Application modules are a high-level means of thinking about the available business process functionality encapsulated in an SAP R/3 system. You can envision the R/3 system as consisting of a series of application modules that support all of a company's business transactions and that are integrated interactively. With this integration, a change of data in one application module will automatically update the data in all other application modules that use that data. All the application modules have a common architecture and user interface. That is, the screens and

FIGURE 1.2
Application Modules Identify Functional Business-Area Processing

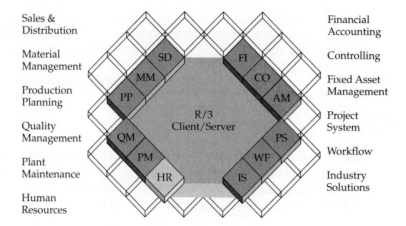

menus provide the same "look-and-feel" for the end user to navigate the system. Each application module consists of those best business practice functions that are used for processing the business transactions assigned to a particular module. As illustrated in **Figure 1.2,** the primary application modules are Financial Accounting, Controlling, Fixed Asset Management, Sales & Distribution, Material Management, Production Planning, Quality Management, Plant Maintenance, Human Resources, Project System, Workflow, and Industry Solutions. While each application module represents a business area's overall set of transactions, these are not actually distinct program code modules. Rather, each application module is a lower-level coordinated collection of related **business process procedures** (BPPs) that are processed at the atomic level. That is, the BPPs are applied to support a particular module's function business area. (Actually, as you will learn later in this book, the atomic-level BPPs are shared, as appropriate, among the various module areas to furnish the high level of functional integration provided by the SAP R/3 System.) To gain an overall view of the system's available processing capabilities, you will find it helpful to think about the R/3 Enterprise as consisting of the application modules.

In **Figure 1.2,** Workflow and Industry Solutions are known as the Common Systems. Workflow integrates the functionality of the other application modules, whereas Industry Solutions provides the functionality for the integration of add-ons to the R/3 System that are developed to meet specific processing needs of a particular industry, such as those found in banking or used by utility companies. Industry Solutions complement the extensive set of business processes and functions included with the standard R/3 System. A number of these solutions have been developed by other software vendors and consulting companies.

The application modules share data through the R/3 database, which is contained within the "R/3 Client/Server" function shown in **Figure 1.2.** When data is entered for any one of the modules, it is placed in the R/3 database and is immediately available to all other R/3 application modules.

Process Integration

The SAP R/3 Enterprise software integrates the core business processes found in many organizations through a very comprehensive set of BPPs available within the various application modules. Key business processes can be used to illustrate the arrangement of the fundamental SCM processes, which follow the customer

FIGURE 1.3
Integrated Business
Processes for SCM

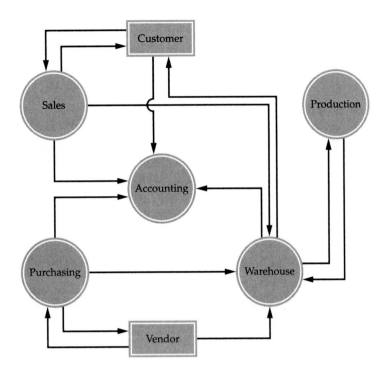

order-to-cash cycle of a business. These fundamental integrated business processes for the SCM are illustrated in **Figure 1.3.** In this figure, circles represent the primary processing departments within the organization, whereas rectangles represent the external interactions with the company's customers and vendors. The key activities and interrelationships among Sales, Purchasing, Production, Warehouse, and Accounting are described next.

Suppose this integrated SCM processing is initiated by a customer sales order. The sales order is then processed through warehousing, shipping, billing, and production. A request for quotation (RFQ) is issued to purchase needed materials for production. This RFQ is converted to a purchase requisition, with the materials received and placed in the warehouse for subsequent use in the production process. Production occurs following a production cycle. Payment of the vendor's invoice in accounting uses the SAP three-way check for logistics invoice verification.

The sales process includes these steps:

1. Enter a sales order from a customer.
2. Create a delivery document from the sales order.
3. Issue pick, pack, and ship documents for the warehouse.
4. Prepare the customer billing from the delivery confirmation from the warehouse that is sent to the customer and transferred to accounts receivable.

The production process includes these steps:

1. Issue a transfer order from the transfer requirement from a bill of materials (BOM).
2. Create, release, and stage production of the product.
3. Confirm the transfer order and create a goods issue from the warehouse to move semi-finished goods from the warehouse to production.

4. Create and run a production order to produce the product.
5. Confirm the production order when the finished product is complete.
6. Create a goods receipt to place the finished product into the warehouse.

The warehouse management process includes these steps:

1. Create a goods receipt for the receipt of goods in interim storage.
2. Issue a transfer order to move the goods to a physical storage location.
3. Create a control cycle record with a transfer requirement converted to a transfer order.
4. Confirm the transfer order when the goods are moved to interim storage where production takes control of these materials.
5. Create a goods receipt for finished goods received from production in interim storage.
6. Create a transfer order from a transfer requirement to move the finished goods to a physical storage location.
7. Confirm the transfer order when the goods have been moved to storage.
8. Receive a transfer order produced directly from the delivery document from the sale order.
9. Confirm the transfer order when goods are picked and packed for shipping from interim storage.
10. Post a goods issue with reference to the delivery document when goods are shipped from interim storage.

The purchasing process includes these steps:

1. Create a purchase requisition for needed materials from production.
2. Issue an RFQ for the needed materials to selected vendors.
3. Receive the RFQs from the vendors.
4. Select a vendor.
5. Issue a purchase order to the vendor with reference to the quotation.
6. Issue a goods receipt upon arrival of the goods at the warehouse with an accounting document and a material document produced.
7. After receipt of the goods and upon receipt of the vendor's invoice, verify the vendor's invoice and produce an accounting document for accounts payable posting.

These steps reinforce the integration of the business processes for SCM. All these processes (**Figure 1.3**) and more are integrated in the SAP R/3 System application modules. This process integration is examined in more detail in *Chapter 4— Business Processes.*

Client/Server Architecture

SAP R/3 is a three-tier client/server architecture that is organized as a database server, an application server, and a client. The client is a desktop component that runs on the computer of each end user. The database server stores all the data for the business transactions, the data that specifies the configuration of the R/3 Systems, and all the program code that implements the best business practices. The application server is where the business processes are actually executed using data obtained from the database server and from the client of the end user. The "3" in R/3 specifies these three pieces or levels of the client server architecture. (The "3" does *not* indicate that this is release 3. Actually, R/3 has undergone a number of different releases that include release 2.2, 3.0d, 3.0f, 3.1h, 4.0a, 4.0b, 4.5, 4.6b, 4.6c, and 4.7.)

The three-tier architecture makes R/3 a flexible system. Without changing the R/3 software, additional database servers can be added. Or, if processing is a bottleneck, then more application servers can be added as more application modules are used. This scalability allows the system to grow as more end users are added. With more end users, another application server can be added to handle the increased processing demands of those users.

In the R/3 architecture, an application server is capable of running *any* of the application modules. Because the application server requests the processing code from the database server, the same application server may be processing transactions from several different application modules concurrently, such as working on transactions from both the Finance module and the Sales & Distribution module.

Customization

Customization is the process of **configuring** the R/3 application modules to match the available SAP business processes with an organization's workflow processes. This is where the application modules are set up to meet the transaction processing requirements of a specific business enterprise. Configuring encompasses selecting and specifying the R/3 business functions to represent an organization's legal structure, reporting requirements, and business workflow processes. During configuration a generic SAP R/3 business model is transformed into an organization's specific business model by mapping the business process of the organization into the available SAP R/3 business functions (the BPPs). The R/3 Reference Model is provided through the SAP **Reference IMG** (Implementation Guide), which is a built-in tool that is included to support these configuration activities. The Reference Model contains a complete description of the business function BPPs contained in the R/3 application modules. The selection and combination of these business processes from the available processes is what makes one R/3 installation unique from another. How the business processes are selected and configured gives one business using SAP R/3 a competitive advantage relative to other businesses in the same industry that are also using the R/3 System. Customization is explored in more detail in several of the chapters that follow.

Quick Check

1. True or false: Enterprise software is stand-alone modules that handle the transaction processing requirements of individual business units.
2. _____ software is the generation of integrated business software that preceded today's more integrated enterprise software.
3. _____ is the creation of entirely new and more effective business processes, without regard for what has gone before.
4. SAP R/3 is _____ transaction processing software that supports an organization's value chain.
5. True or false: The R/3 application modules are integrated interactively.

6. The _____ business processes are implemented with transaction processing systems that are most concerned with the day-to-day needs of conducting the affairs of a business.

7. The three-tier client/server architecture is important in providing which three features of the R/3 System?

8. True or false: An R/3 application module is the same as an R/3 application server.

9. _____ is the process of configuring the R/3 application modules.

Chapter 2

Navigation and Systems Operation

SAP Window Elements

Navigation and systems operation control the use of the R/3 System that focuses on the processing of business transactions. The computer screen displays the SAP Window in which you carry out the various transactions of the R/3 System. The SAP R/3 Logon Screen is the first screen that appears. This screen enables you to enter the client, user name, password, and language. In the R/3 System the **client** is the highest level at which data is organized, and this entry specifies the version of data that is accessed during this R/3 logon. The language, also known as the user's logon language, specifies the language in which the titles for screen fields, the headings on reports, and user messages will be displayed. Log on in English and all these elements are displayed in English; logging on in Spanish results in the display of these elements in Spanish. The SAP R/3 System is designed to handle this multilanguage processing efficiently.

After you log on, the main SAP R/3 window or display screen appears. This is the SAP Easy Access screen, which became available in Release 4.6. The primary elements of this window are indicated in **Figure 2.1.** The Title Bar, Menu Bar, and Status Bar are similar to other Windows applications, with these elements displayed in the selected logon language. The Function Icons and the Application Toolbar are similar to the toolbars used with other Windows applications such as Microsoft Word and Excel. The Command Field is a shortcut feature of R/3 that allows you to enter an R/3 transaction code and to immediately initiate that transaction. This feature provides an expert-user mode for bypassing menu selections. The function icons on the Standard Toolbar include those for Save, Back, Exit, Cancel, Screen Movement, and Help. The Back function is used to return to the previous screen, whereas the Exit function is used to return to a higher-level menu screen.

The Favorites area of the SAP Easy Access menu enables you to create a customized set of frequently used menu choices. These can be links to (1) selected R/3 transactions, (2) selected Web sites, or (3) other non-SAP application systems. Here, the Favorites area provides a convenient launch pad for frequently accessed transactions and other links.

FIGURE 2.1
SAP Window
Elements

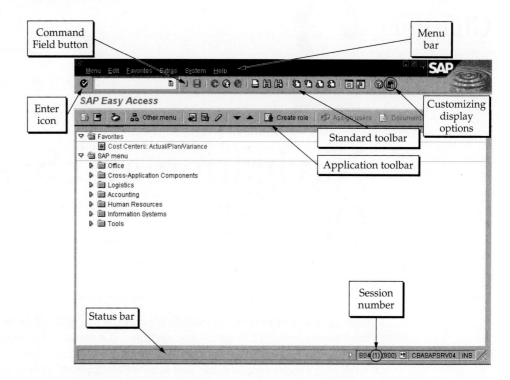

From the Systems menu you can change default settings such as the date and decimal display formats. For example, the date can be displayed as MM/DD/YYYY or DD/MM/YYYY, or the decimal indicator can be either a period or a comma.

The R/3 System supports multiple sessions, so you can have more than one SAP Window open at once. You can then toggle between windows or arrange the panes so that multiple transactions can be viewed concurrently. This can be useful in looking at related data from different transaction screens. Part II of this book introduces you to the navigation and execution of available R/3 System transactions.

While much of the navigation from screen to screen is very similar to Microsoft Word and Excel navigation, each of the business process transactions appears much more structured, with a prespecified movement from one transaction screen to the next. You enter and view data on these screens. The data you enter may create new data for inclusion in the database, such as a customer order. However, your freedom in processing a transaction is much more limited than is the more free-form creation of a letter or report in Word. Learning to interact with the SAP R/3 System as an end user means that you have the ability to select an appropriate business transaction and complete the sequence of screens for that transaction. End users do not create new transactions or reports; they merely work with these existing components of the R/3 System. This introduction to navigation and systems operation provides you with a beginning understanding of this interaction with the R/3 System.

Online Help

The R/3 System has extensive help facilities provided through field-level help, pop-up window help, a glossary, and a comprehensive R/3 Library of help documentation with hypertext. **Search Help** is a query tool used to find specific information used in completing transactions. This field-level help is often available by use of a list arrow or the F4 key to display possible field values or match-codes. A **matchcode** allows you to locate the key of a particular database record (e.g., the account number) by entering information contained in the record. A list of records matching the specifications is then displayed. Pop-up window help or the shortcut menu displays a list of the available function keys and their actions. This list is context sensitive for the current screen and menu. The **glossary** provides definitions for fields in the R/3 System, such as the definition for the "material number." The R/3 Library contains in-depth descriptions of the application modules and their functions within the R/3 System. Prior to Release 4.0 the R/3 Library was provided by use of the Microsoft Winhelp feature. Beginning with Release 4.0 the R/3 Library is also available in an HTML format. These various Online Help features of the R/3 System provide considerable information to help you understand the system's operation, once you have a general idea of the R/3 modules and their transactions.

Change Material Master

Operation of the R/3 System can be demonstrated by changing the material master record. For example, the MM/PP status can be revised, where the material master (MM) and production planning (PP) status indicate the use of a material in business functions. This status determines the conditions for which a warning or an error message appears, such as blocking the issuing of procurements by an end user in the warehouse.

SAP AG has evolved a common way of specifying menu selections: The symbol → is used to indicate that you point to or click the next menu item. In the SAP Easy Access navigation pane, you click the expand arrow at the left of a menu item or double-click the menu item name to expand the lower-level menu. Using this method, the menu selections for changing the material master are specified as follows:

Select **Logistics** → **Materials Management** → **Material Master** →

The Material Master menu opens for continuing selections.

Select **Material** → **Change**

The Change menu appears with the lowest-level items for your selection.

Double-click **Immediately**

Because Immediately is on the lowest-level menu, you double-click that menu item to select it. These selections result in the display of the Change Material (Initial Screen). (From now on, when one of a series of screens associated with a master screen is mentioned, such as the initial screen of the master "Change Material" screen, a colon (:) will precede it; for example, the "Change Material: Initial Screen.")

You enter the Material number on the Change Material: Initial Screen and are then ready to work with the data for the specified material. The data that appears is specified from the Select view(s) button on the Application toolbar. When you select the Purchasing view, the data that is relevant to the purchasing process appears on the Change Material screen. This includes the General data that is appropriate for all views together with the purchasing-specific data.

The Plant-sp. matl status or MM/PP status appears under the General data section of the Change Material screen as shown in **Figure 2.2.** A list arrow for this field indicates that available values may be displayed for selection in a separate dialog

FIGURE 2.2
Change Material:
Master Screen

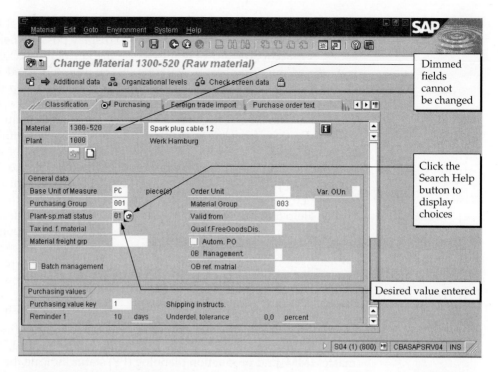

box. When you click the list arrow, a dialog box appears, and you can select the desired status from the available list. Upon exiting from this screen, you are prompted to save the data. During the save operation the change is completed to the Material Master record in the R/3 database, and a confirmation message appears in the status bar. On exiting from the Material Master screen, you return to the main R/3 Menu for the next processing activity.

The values displayed in **Figure 2.2** for Motor Sports International (MSI) are provided from the IDES training data. Because the training data is a preconfigured R/3 System, these values were available for selection and display. Otherwise, all the data for the Material would need to be entered before a change could be made. Selecting and entering data values is a typical part of using the R/3 System to process business transactions. Recall that working with the R/3 System is not as free-form as working in Word or Excel. So, in learning to navigate and operate the SAP R/3 System, you frequently will need to enter values for existing materials, customers, and vendors; you cannot be creative with the value you use. While you can try values on your own, much of the data you want to work on already resides within the IDES training data. As a result, trying your own values will often lead to a condition of no available data. Therefore, you should use the specific values as provided in the examples in this book. Although you may at times find this frustrating, you will have a good understanding and command of available data values when you eventually work with these transactions on your job. Following the examples outlined in this book will enable you to gain an understanding of this processing in enterprise software in general and in SAP R/3 specifically.

Display Planned Changes

A change, such as that made to the Material Master, can be made immediately, as illustrated in the previous section, or it can be scheduled for implementation at a future date. If a number of Material Master records were being revised because of a change in the business processes of an organization, it might take several days to enter all the data for these changes. In that situation, it might be desirable for all the changes to take effect on the same day. A **planned change** is a transaction that is scheduled for a specified date in the future. Once a planned change transaction has been entered, that change can be displayed for review. This is accomplished by displaying planned changes.

The menu selections for displaying planned changes are as follows:

Select **Logistics** → **Materials Management** → **Material Master** →

The Material Master menu opens for continuing selections.

Select **Material** → **Display Changes**

The Planned Changes menu appears with the lowest-level items for your selection.

Double-click **Scheduled Changes**

Note: If your SAP Easy Access menu remains expanded from a prior selection, you can just continue to make lower-level selections without beginning from the top-level menu. So, if you did make the selection for the Change Material Master, you would have all the menus expanded through the Material menu. You could then just open the Display Changes menu and select Planned Changes. That is, you need not expand an already expanded menu. On the other hand, you may find that you have so many lower-level menus open that it is more difficult for you to understand your current menu expansion. In that situation, you might close some of the other expanded menus to make it easier to understand your current location in the SAP Easy Access menu structure.

These selections cause the Display Planned Changes: Initial Screen to display. In the Selection parameters section, the "Changes scheduled until" field enables you to enter a date for displaying the planned changes until the specified date. You can type the date directly, or you can use the Search Help list button for this field to display the Calendar dialog box from which a date can be specified by the selection of the year, month, and day. Selecting the Choose button completes the Calendar entry, and the Execute button on the Application toolbar is selected to produce the Display Change Documents report with a list of all planned changes for the material specified by the Material field in the Selection parameters section of the Display Planned Changes: Initial Screen. You can double-click any of the planned changes listed in the report to drill down to the details of that change. The Exit button on the Standard toolbar is used to return to the main R/3 menu for the next processing action.

Create Purchase Order

A purchase order is created within the Logistics modules from the Create Purchase Order screens. The data used for the purchase order is the MSI data from the training database. This provides important data values that include the vendor number, purchasing organization, purchasing group, and material. Once again, the training database provides many of the data values that are used. Without this training database, all the supporting data for this transaction would need to be entered into the R/3 System. The menu selections for the create purchase order process are specified as follows:

Select **Logistics** → **Materials Management** → **Purchasing** →

The Purchasing menu opens for continuing selections.

Select **Purchase Order** → **Create**

The Create menu appears with the lowest-level transactions items for your selection.

Double-click **Vendor Unknown**

These selections display the Create Purchase Order: Initial Screen. Values are specified for the fields Order type, Purchase order date, Delivery date, Purchasing group, and Plant. The values may be typed or selected from an available dialog box using Search Help. Here, the Organizational data represents the organizational structure for MSI. Once the purchasing group is entered, click the Item overview button to display the Create Purchase Order: Overview of Requisition Items screen where the Material, Quantity requested, Delivery date, Material group, and Plant are entered. Also, when you click the Enter button, you will obtain the value for the Short text description and the Unit of measure from the database. Then click the Enter button to complete the specification for the first item of the purchase order and to display the Requisition Item screen. Dimmed fields, such as the Material, Material group, and Plant, cannot be changed from this screen. A value on this screen, such as the Unit of Measure, is a value that is entered when the material is initially placed in the R/3 database. The Release Strategy button displays a dialog box that requests a Commitment item number, which is completed with the Continue button. Next, the Save as requisition button on the Application toolbar is used to save the purchase order as a requisition. This completes the Create Purchase Order process. The Exit button on the Standard toolbar is used to return to the SAP Easy Access menu.

Find Transaction Code

An R/3 **transaction code** is typically a sequence of four alphanumeric characters that uniquely identifies a screen and report as a task or transaction in the R/3 System. A transaction is immediately initiated by entering the transaction code in the Command Field and pressing the Enter key. To use the advanced, shortcut feature of the R/3 System, you need to know the transaction code for the transactions you want to perform. The transaction code for the current transaction, that is, the currently displayed R/3 screen, is found as follows:

Select **System** → **Status**

The System Status dialog box displays with the transaction code appearing in the Transaction field of the SAP data section of that dialog box. This is a code such as "ME25" to create a purchase order. All the fields in this dialog box are dimmed as a reminder that these values cannot be changed by the user. Or, the transaction code can be displayed with each of the transactions on the SAP Easy Access menu. The codes and transactions can be displayed as follows:

From the SAP Easy Access menu,

Select **Extras** → **Settings**

Then click the **Display technical name** check box to enable this feature.

The transaction code is now displayed with its respective transaction name.

Any transaction codes that begin with "Y" or "Z" are user-defined transactions that were created specifically for a particular business using the Advanced Business Application Programming (ABAP) language that is an integral part of the

R/3 System. All other transaction codes are those reserved for transactions provided by SAP AG with the R/3 System as the application modules.

Once the transaction code is known, it can be entered in the Command Field for direct access to that transaction. If you precede the transaction code with **/n**, such as **/nMM15**, then the specified transaction is the next screen opened in the current session. If you precede the transaction code with **/o**, such as **/oMM15**, then a new session is opened for the transaction. Use of the **/o** results in multiple sessions so that you can readily toggle between these sessions or resize the transaction windows so both transaction screens can be viewed at once. Alternatively, you can include the transaction in the Favorites menu of the SAP Easy Access menu. This permits you to readily launch those transactions that you frequently use.

Menu paths and transaction codes are alternatives for executing the same R/3 transactions. Whether you use the R/3 System menu paths, illustrated previously, or the transaction code, is a matter of your preference in interacting with the R/3 System to perform the desired task.

Quick Check

1. List the two required fields for the R/3 logon procedure other than the User and Password.

2. User _____ are default values for frequently used fields.

3. _____ are used to find field values in completing R/3 transactions.

4. You should click the _____ of an R/3 transaction screen to show all possible field values.

5. _____ contains documentation that describes processing activities in the various R/3 application modules.

6. You can use _____ to obtain sample data and processing steps for performing R/3 transactions.

7. After selecting System from the Menu Bar and then selecting _____, you can find the transaction code for an R/3 screen.

Chapter 3

Application Modules

R/3 Integration

SAP R/3 integrates transaction data among the various business functions in supply chain processing. Transaction data is entered where the data is initially created in the business processes—from the receipt of a customer order to the delivery of that order to the customer. Once entered, the data is available for use with all other transaction processing events along the supply chain, such as the purchasing of materials and the production of goods or services to fulfill the order. That is, a change in the data from one SAP R/3 application module will result in an automatic update of that data when it is used in the other application modules involved. Shared data expedites transaction processing and the response to customer requests. This availability and use of transaction data provides a competitive advantage with customers. All R/3 application modules have a common architecture and user interface that provide the same look-and-feel and screen navigation, as shown in Chapter 2.

The application modules represent a conceptual collection of R/3 best business practice functions. At the lowest, or atomic, level of the R/3 Systems, **business process procedures** (BPPs) are the actual program elements that provide the functionality of the R/3 System. Many of these BPPs are used by more than one of the application modules. So, no single program module implements the various applications of SD, MM, PP, and so on. Rather, it is the implementation of appropriate BPPs that provides the desired business functionality for each of these application modules. Nonetheless, it is useful to think about the R/3 System from the viewpoint of application modules, because this provides a high-level perspective of how the various atomic-level program elements can be integrated to support these commonly recognized higher-level business functions.

The transaction data resides in central databases for companywide integration that provides crucial control and coordination. Application link enabling (ALE) technology facilitates the transfer of standard business messages between processes and supports the integration of multiple business partners into common business processes of the central databases. The Internet extends this supply chain integration outside the boundaries of the business itself to encompass vendors and customers. Using the Internet, businesses can more readily exchange and share transaction information for the real-time processing of business transactions along the entire supply chain.

Financial Modules

The R/3 financial modules include the application areas of Financial Accounting (FI), Controlling (CO), Asset Management (AM), and Project System (PS). The FI application module is designed for automated management and external reporting of general ledger, accounts receivable, accounts payable, and other subledger accounts based on a user-defined chart of accounts. The CO application module represents the company's flow of cost and revenue in the management of internal operations that include cost center accounting, internal order accounting, project accounting, product costing analysis, profitability analysis, profit center accounting, and activity-based accounting. The AM application module is designed to manage and supervise individual aspects of fixed assets including plant maintenance and repair, asset replacement, and depreciation. The PS application module supports the planning, control, and monitoring of long-term, highly complex projects with defined goals. It accelerates work and data flows while reducing routine tasks. If a company does not need the project management provided by this module, then it could decide not to implement this module. This is an example of how companies can select the modules they need from those provided as part of the R/3 System. All modules do not need to be implemented. However, the FI and CO modules are nearly always included in the implementation because they provide the chart of accounts for the basic accounting functionality that is required to support the other modules.

Common System Modules

The common system modules include Workflow (WF) and Industry Solutions (IS). The WF application module links the other integrated SAP R/3 application modules with cross-application technologies, tools, and services. These services are implemented with the R/3 document management system (DMS) that is comprised of several features for managing documents that are stored in the R/3 System. The DMS makes documents available on a companywide basis and links them to SAP objects from the other application areas, such as material masters, change masters, and production resources and tools. The entire life cycle of a document is processed from initial document creation through document storage. WF provides this support for linking all the other modules. The business processes are automated according to predefined procedures and rules specified with WF. As events occur that trigger a process, the Workflow Manager automatically initiates a Workflow item. Using rules for the business process, the Workflow Manager routes the item to the appropriate role, such as a person or location for continued processing or review. WF is configured to automatically trigger Workflow items by data or exceptions. For example, as a user completes a transaction, an **intermediate document** (IDOC) is frequently created with the number of the IDOC displayed for the user's reference in the status bar of the R/3 screen. The data from that IDOC is then ready for use by the other application modules. IDOC processing involves various programs that (1) send IDOCs to a second module, (2) receive IDOCs from a second module, and (3) process status information from a second module.

The IS module facilitates the combination of the SAP R/3 application modules with additional industry-specific functionality to provide a total solution for a business. That is, an IS is an add-on to the basic functionality of the R/3 System.

The IS system enhances the overall SAP installation to meet the specialized requirements of an organization in that industry sector. Examples of industry solutions include aerospace and defense, automotive, banking, chemicals, consumer products, healthcare, high tech and electronics, insurance, gas and oil, pharmaceuticals, public sector, retail, telecommunications, and utilities. The public sector components include colleges and universities, government entities, and not-for-profit organizations. The efforts are provided through Centers of Expertise (COEs) both within SAP AG and through agreements and partnerships with other developers. A consulting firm providing SAP support will frequently create one or more industry solutions and then specialize in the implementation of SAP R/3 in those industries where it has developed the IS.

Human Resources Module

The R/3 Human Resources (HR) module is a complete integrated system for supporting the planning and control of personnel activities, including those for payroll and benefits. Key elements of the HR module include personnel administration, benefits, recruitment, time management, incentive wages, business trip management, payroll, training and events management, personnel development, and workforce development. Data from the HR module is integrated with the other modules. For example, planned personnel costs in the HR module are transferred to the FI and CO modules. A **personnel event** occurs when data is entered on a transaction screen, and the R/3 System updates all relevant data with control access managed for sensitive personal data.

Logistic Modules

The R/3 Logistic modules include Plant Maintenance (PM), Quality Management (QM), Production Planning (PP), Materials Management (MM), and Sales and Distribution (SD). The PM module supports the planning, processing, and completion of plant maintenance tasks. It tracks maintenance costs and resources to provide information that facilitates decision making about plant maintenance. Key elements of the PM module include maintenance notification, maintenance planning, and maintenance bills of material. The QM module provides quality control and information systems support for quality planning, inspection, and control for manufacturing, costing, and procurement. The PP module is used to plan and control the manufacturing activities of a company. Key elements of the PP module include bills of materials (BOMs), routings, work centers, master production scheduling (MPS), material requirements planning (MRP), shop floor control (SFC), and repetitive manufacturing. The MM module supports the procurement and delivery functions occurring in day-to-day business operations of supply chain management. Key elements of the MM module include purchasing, inventory management, reorder point processing, invoice verification, material valuation, vendor evaluation, and warehouse management. The SD module helps to optimize all the tasks and activities carried out in sales, delivery, and billing of supply chain management. Key elements of the SD module include pre-sales support, inquiry processing, sales order processing, quotation processing, delivery processing, and billing.

FIGURE 3.1
Web Application
Server

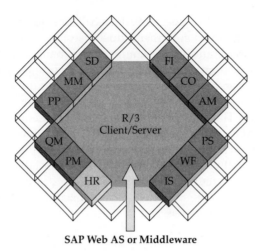

SAP Web AS or Middleware

Web Application Server

The SAP **Web Application Server** (Web AS) is the **middleware** or central piece of the R/3 System as indicated in **Figure 3.1.** The Web AS, previously known as the SAP Basis, ensures that all the SAP application modules are integrated and platform-independent. This makes the application modules independent of the system interfaces of the operating system, database system, and communication system used to ensure the optimal handling of business transactions. It provides the functionality that supports the integration of BPPs for the R/3 application modules. This standard operating environment supports processing all of a company's business transactions, regardless of the module containing the transaction, and includes the enabling features for the client/server architecture, the application architecture, and the system communication. The Web AS includes the ABAP programming language and a business-strength Java engine. ABAP is the tool used to build individual BPPs for the application modules of the R/3 Enterprise System, including those provided by SAP and the industry solutions developed by third-party vendors. However, with its new Java engine, the door is open to future developments in either Java or ABAP.

The SAP Web AS is a component of SAP NetWeaver, which provides additional tools and functionalities for several SAP business software packages. The Web AS is described in more detail in Chapter 5.

R/3 System Benefits

A primary benefit of the R/3 System is its integration. Processes, data, and organizational elements are integrated so that operational, financial, and managerial requirements are satisfied simultaneously through the use of a common database. Applications are integrated so that there is one point of data entry and so that consistency exists for the users across applications. Technical integration provides for online, real-time data editing and updating, for the elimination of redundant data, and for data integrity. The R/3 System provides a complete business solution across all business functions for strategic and operational control of an organization. This facilitates an enterprisewide solution, with one system supporting global business and accounting practices, standardized business processes across the organization, and multiple organization structures per business process. Interactive processing is handled so that business transactions are processed as logical units of work (LUWs). This helps the management of the database to preserve data consistency and to observe business requirements while performing updates asynchronously. This feature facilitates processing multiple users' input interactively as it provides simultaneous changes to the database.

Through the Web AS, the SAP R/3 System is an open system that promotes portability by the use of industry standards for interfaces to other, non-SAP applications. This open system supports the interoperability of applications, data, and user interfaces. Industry standards implemented in the R/3 System include TCP/IP (a network communications protocol), EDI (a mechanism for the electronic exchange of business data between organizations), OLE (an integration of personal computer applications), and Open Interfaces (an interface to specialized applications such as bar coding).

A number of features included in the R/3 System support its worldwide usage. This functionality consists of comprehensive multicurrency translation, multiple language support, customized reports for individual countries, multicompany organizations, local technical and consulting support in most major countries, and country-specific features such as government reporting and taxation.

Overall, this functionality results in a flexible system for processing business transactions. Organizations customize the available business modules to obtain their particular fit with the best business practices. The Web AS provides necessary interfaces to incorporate external software and unique development tools for customization and applications development. The R/3 System, through its three-tier client/server architecture, is scalable and runs on multiple hardware platforms to accommodate different size organizations, as well as to respond to business combinations and future growth. The R/3 System can be reconfigured to adjust to changes in the way an organization does business in the future. The Web AS supports the development of customized screens, processing, and reports to enhance the functionality of the SAP-provided application modules or to create the industry-specific solutions.

Business Framework

The business framework indicates the future strategic direction for the SAP R/3 System product architecture. The purpose is to provide a standards-based environment through which SAP R/3 and third-party software components can dynamically interoperate. The framework reveals SAP AG's plan to deliver new capabilities, components, and technology to its customers in a continuous manner that is independent of conventional upgrade release cycles. The business framework encompasses the business process components, the interface technology, and the integration technology. Prior to Release 4.0 of the R/3 System, as new features were added such as IDOCs, EDI, and Internet capabilities, a new release of the System was frequently implemented. Companies undertook the entire release in an "all or nothing" situation. The purpose of the framework is to allow companies using the R/3 System to (1) reduce the time to deploy and continuously improve business processes, (2) dynamically reconfigure live R/3 Systems with no business disruption, (3) improve system maintainability by using components on different release cycles, and (4) choose complementary software from other vendors to interoperate within the R/3 System.

Primary building blocks of the Business Framework architecture include business components, business objects, and business application program interfaces (BAPIs). Business components are software modules that collaborate via standard interfaces, such as the Logistics application modules. An SAP business object, such as a customer order, vendor, or employee, is used in the SAP business processes. These business objects combine data and processing functionality in the R/3 System. BAPIs are language-independent interfaces that provide a standard method to integrate SAP business components and third-party applications. In this manner the overall future of the SAP R/3 System is designated through the Business Framework.

Quick Check

1. True or false: R/3 encompasses *all* the information processing requirements of every business.
2. _____ embraces *all* the business processes from the receipt of a customer order to the delivery of that order to the customer.
3. The R/3 _____ integrates *all* the application modules and implements the client/server architecture.
4. Application integration provides for _____ point of data entry, which results in _____ for the user across applications.
5. A benefit of SAP R/3 System is the _____ business processes used across the organization.
6. True or false: R/3 incorporates unique development tools for customizing the different application modules.
7. The _____ is a strategy that guides the future development of SAP R/3 Enterprise System.

Chapter  4

Business Processes

Business Process Integration

Most companies can be viewed as consisting of four primary, "big picture" business processes. These are (1) customer order management (sales), (2) manufacturing planning and execution (production), (3) procurement (purchasing), and (4) financial/management accounting and reporting. The business processes are integrated through transactions that share common data as indicated in **Figure 4.1.** The Financial/Management Accounting and Reporting process transcends the other three business processes because it is the mechanism for providing the desired accounting controls for the various transactions. In processing transactions in the R/3 System, an **order** is a fundamental document. It describes the work to be done in terms of which task is to be carried out and when, what is needed to carry out this task, and how the costs are to be settled. Examples of an order (**Figure 4.1**) include a sales order, a purchase order, a planned order, a production order, and a shipping order. This section examines these main business processes together with a number of the documents or transactions that implement them.

The four main business processes are handled within the R/3 System by the integrated use of the R/3 application modules as indicated by the matrix shown in **Figure 4.2.**

The R/3 application modules implement various transactions (BPPs) that carry out the functionality of a particular application module. These transactions ultimately support the business processes for an organization. The integration of some of the more common transactions among the business processes is indicated in **Figure 4.3.** This integration reinforces the need for the R/3 integrated database so the data is readily shared. Entering the data for one business process makes it available for use in other processes. For example, the Goods Receipt transactions affect the manufacturing, procurement, and financial management business processes. Here, a goods receipt also represents an "order" because it produces a document used in a similar manner within the R/3 System as a purchase order or a sales order.

Motor Sports International

Motor Sports International (MSI) is a case example created by SAP AG for use in training. MSI manufactures and sells motorcycles and related parts at multiple plant locations. The MSI data is useful in illustrating the features, architecture, and

FIGURE 4.1 Integrated Business Processes and Documents

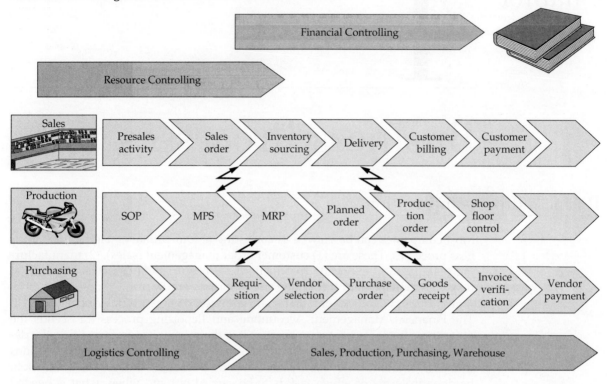

FIGURE 4.2 Business Process Integration Through R/3 Application Modules

R/3 Application Module — Business Process	Manufacturing	Customer Order Management	Procurement	Financial Management
Sales & Distribution (SD)	X	X		
Materials Mgmt. (MM)	X	X	X	
Production Planning (PP)	X	X	X	
Quality Management (QM)	X			
Plant Maintenance (PM)			X	
Human Resources (HR)	X			
Financial Accounting (FI)	X	X	X	X
Controlling (CO)	X	X	X	X
Fixed Asset Mgmt. (AM)				X

integration of the SAP R/3 System and is part of the IDES (Internet Documentation and Education System) training data. This training database is vital in examining the SAP R/3 Enterprise software. Because the transactions and data are so complex, it is necessary to have a system that already has some data available for examination and use. Otherwise, it would be extremely arduous to create all the data needed to begin effectively examining the R/3 System. The MSI case and its

FIGURE 4.3 R/3 Transactions Implement Business Processes

R/3 Module Functionality \\ Business Process	Manufacturing	Customer Order Management	Procurement	Financial Management
MRP	X	X	X	
Purchase Order			X	
Goods Receipt	X		X	X
Planned Order	X			
Production Order	X	X		X
Shop Floor Control	X		X	X
Sales Order	X	X		
Customer Billing		X		X
Financial Mgmt. Acctg.				X
Financial Mgmt. Report				X

related IDES data are referenced in subsequent sections of this book as appropriate for illustrating the application and use of the R/3 System.

Organizational Elements

The organizational elements are a mechanism for representing a company's organizational structure in the R/3 System. The organizational structure specifies how the data of the business processes is related for the purpose of managing a company. Data in the R/3 System is entered, stored, and reported based on the organizational elements. So, an organizational structure is critical to the configuration of an R/3 System. Usually, organizational elements transcend the business processes and application modules. For example, a company code, which is at a top level of the R/3 organization structure, is used by Financial Accounting, Materials Management, Human Resources, Sales and Distribution, and other application modules.

Several of the SAP organizational elements are used with MSI. A **client** is a legally and organizationally independent unit at the highest level of the SAP R/3 System. This client is a required organizational element that specifies the primary arrangement of data within the R/3 database. A **company** is an independent legal entity within a client. For example, MSI has two legal entities: MSI US (3000) and MSI Canada (4000). A **business area** is used to produce internal balance sheets and profit/loss statements. For example, MSI has two business areas that are arranged as Motorcycles (02) and Accessories (90). A **purchasing organization** is a unit that negotiates general conditions of acquiring materials and services for one or more plants. MSI has one purchasing organization in the United States. A **plant** is an organizational unit within a company that corresponds to a location, facility, or branch. Plants are used by all Logistics applications. MSI is organized with two plants—one in New York (3000) and the other in Seattle (3400). Both plants are served by the same purchasing organization. A **storage location** is used to distinguish an area within a plant for inventory purposes. A **sales organization** is

FIGURE 4.4
Organizational
Elements Available
in R/3 System

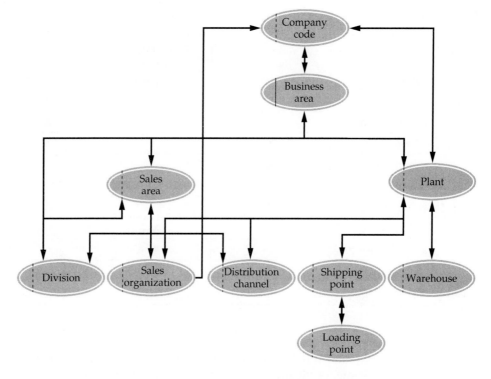

responsible for negotiating sales conditions and for distributing materials and services. MSI has one sales organization in the United States. A **distribution channel** is an organizational unit that determines how materials reach a customer. For MSI, Retail Sales (03) is a distribution channel. A **division** is an organizational unit based on the responsibility for sales or profits from salable materials or services. For example, MSI uses divisions to monitor product-line profitability with separate divisions for Motorcycles (02) and Accessories (90).

The overall arrangement of the organizational elements is illustrated in an organizational diagram (**Figure 4.4**). These are the available organizational units in the R/3 System. They must be selected and specified before any data is initially entered for any of the R/3 transactions, which occurs as an R/3 configuration activity that is presented in Chapters 7 and 10. An individual company can then choose how it will use these available organizational units within the company. For example, a commercial airline may identify an individual aircraft as a plant in the R/3 system. Master data is then stored in the R/3 System based upon the selected and specified organizational elements. This master data is used where appropriate across the four business processes.

Customer Order Management

Customer Order Management (COM) is the selling activities including sales order processing, shipping, billing, and cash processing. Data entered for one activity is automatically made available for other activities in this processing. A **sales order** is a document that specifies the material and quantity requested by a particular customer. Shipping involves transfer of the ownership of the goods by creating a delivery document, physically transferring the goods, and recording the goods issue or shipment. Billing and invoicing is the process of requesting payment for the goods shipped to the customer. Cash or payment processing is the recording of the customer's payment, including changes in available credit and accounts receivable and the recording of cash discounts.

Manufacturing Planning and Execution

Manufacturing planning and execution (production or making) encompasses the process of recognizing demand, netting requirements, planning for the production or procurement of materials, and identifying the capacity to satisfy demand. Here, **netting requirements** is calculating and adjusting material stocks to determine available quantities based on any new quantities that have been delivered or are expected to be delivered, less those quantities used in production. The master production schedule (MPS) is a statement of the anticipated build schedule and its impact on the material and capacity requirements plan. For example, MSI creates a plan for a four-month build schedule that considers the shop calendar and current inventory when determining the expected demand on production. Material requirements planning (MRP) plans the gross to net calculation of the material plan. Dependent requirements for materials used in final assembly are determined through a bill of materials (BOM) explosion, which produces a detailed list of requirements for all the individual materials or parts used to make an assembled product. For example, MSI used MRP to match the requirements for parts for all components required to build the planned number of motorcycles per month as determined from the MPS.

Planned order processing produces an order proposal when a deficit is expected in the net requirements for the available quantities of a material in a planning period. This allows the material to be obtained from inventory or scheduled for delivery in time to meet the requirement. A **production order** is the authorization for the shop floor to produce a material. For example, MSI releases a production order to the shop floor to cause the build of the planned number of motorcycles. A **goods issue** is the process of issuing material from the warehouse inventory for use in a production order. MSI issues to the production order all components that are necessary for assembling the motorcycles. A **production order confirmation** is the recording of the actual results of a completed production operation that includes the time used per operation, who did the operation, and the amount of yield and scrap produced. A **production order receipt** acknowledges the arrival of the quantity of goods actually produced into inventory in the warehouse. At MSI the production order receipt causes the value of the quantity of motorcycles in inventory to be updated. The motorcycles are then ready to be shipped to their customers when a customer order is received and processed.

Procurement

Procurement (purchasing or buying) is comprised of requisitioning, vendor sourcing, actual purchase, receiving, and paying for materials and services that are used throughout an organization. That is, the procurement process encompasses the purchasing of goods and services from recognition of the requirement through final vendor payment for those goods and services received. A **purchase requisition** is a document that is used to purchase goods and services and can be created manually or automatically during the MRP process of manufacturing planning and execution. A **purchase order** is a binding contract with a vendor to supply certain materials or services based on specified terms and conditions. For MSI a requisition is converted into a purchase order that is sent to MSI's vendor. A **goods receipt** is a transaction that records the movement of physical materials into inventory in the warehouse. This processing involves matching the quantity and materials received against the purchase order to verify this transaction. The **invoice receipt and verification** process involves receiving the vendor invoice, comparing it with the purchase order and goods receipt, and recording the corresponding liability to the vendor as a financial transaction. The vendor payment process actually completes the payment to the vendor by reducing the liability to the vendor and the company's cash position, recording discounts taken, and disbursing the payment. For MSI, vendor payment completes the activities of ordering mirrors from a vendor, receiving them, and issuing a check that is sent to the vendor.

Financial/Management Accounting and Reporting

Financial/Management Accounting and Reporting refers to the process of planning, recording, and monitoring business transaction events. As shown previously in **Figures 4.1** and **4.2,** the recording actions of this business process take place across the activities of the other three main business processes. That is, each of the other main business processes has links to the Financial/Management Accounting and Reporting process. Major functions of this process are general ledger accounting together with legal (external) and management (internal) reporting. Data of the general ledger is stored following the organization structure, described previously, that accommodates the external and internal reporting requirements. This business process includes a flexible set of tools used to analyze and record financial and management performance. This process takes place when a journal entry is posted and when departmental expenses are reviewed and analyzed. Cost accounting reports are produced, and financial statements are created to satisfy legal reporting requirements. Also, this business process emphasizes the manner in which all four main business processes are integrated and share their data through the common R/3 database.

Quick Check

1. True or false: Because of integration in R/3, a change in the data entered in one application module causes an automatic update of data in other application modules that share that data.
2. List the four value-chain business processes.
3. True or false: A client is the lowest-level organizational unit in the R/3 System.
4. _____ data is records that remain in the database over extended periods and is shared across application modules.
5. List three R/3 application modules included in Customer Order Management.
6. List three R/3 application modules included in Manufacturing Planning and Execution.
7. List three R/3 application modules included in Procurement.
8. List two R/3 application modules included in Financial/Management Accounting and Reporting.
9. List three business processes that use the production order.
10. The _____ transaction is used in transferring the ownership of goods.

Chapter 5

Web Application Server

Technical Architecture

Recall that the SAP R/3 System is a three-tier client/server architecture. This architecture has both a physical and a logical structure. The physical structure of a client/server environment is the connection of two or more computers in a network where there are frequently more client computers than server computers. In this client/server environment a network protocol such as TCP/IP is used in managing the communication between the computers. The logical structure of a client/server environment for an SAP R/3 System divides the computer processing tasks into three areas: presentation, application logic, and data storage. The presentation task is the desktop client that handles the display of information for each user. The SAP R/3 System software manages the processing interaction between these three logical components. Client/server technology facilitates the distribution of the logical tasks among several different physical hardware platforms. It also provides integrated communication between the SAP R/3 System components and the other technologies that include the database management system and the computer operating system as indicated in **Figure 5.1.** The technical architecture of the SAP R/3 System is designed so it will run under most computer operating systems, such as Microsoft Windows NT or UNIX, and to utilize various database management systems, such as Oracle and Informix, on a variety of hardware platforms.

The **SAP Web Application Server** (previously known as the SAP Basis System) is the middleware that provides the processing environment for the R/3 application modules. It handles the **scalability** of the R/3 System, which is the distribution of resources and system components across the three-tier client/server environment. The SAP Web Application Server (SAP Web AS) also provides the **portability** of the R/3 System, which is the ability to run the SAP R/3 System on a variety of hardware and operating system platforms. In addition, the SAP Web AS includes the components that support interfaces to non-SAP products and that provide for the overall administration of the entire R/3 System. For example, managing user logons is an administration activity. In this manner, it is the SAP Web AS that guarantees that all application modules are integrated and platform-independent.

The SAP Web AS is a key software component of SAP NetWeaver. **SAP NetWeaver** is a comprehensive integration and application platform designed to lower the total cost of ownership of a company's various information systems.

FIGURE 5.1
SAP R/3 Technical
Architecture

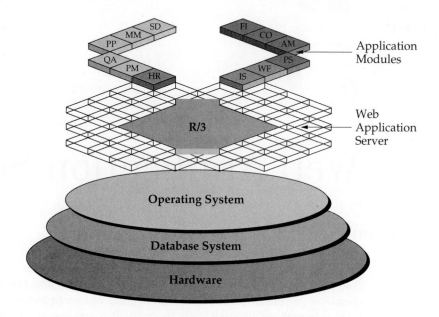

Application
Modules

Web
Application
Server

Operating System

Database System

Hardware

In addition to the SAP Web AS, SAP NetWeaver includes a number of components and tools such as SAP Business Intelligence, SAP Exchange Infrastructure, SAP Master Data Management, SAP Mobile Infrastructure, and SAP Solution Manager. That is, SAP NetWeaver is a comprehensive software platform that includes SAP Web AS as a key critical component. This collection of functionality in NetWeaver embraces Internet standards such as HTTP, XML, and Web services, which make it interoperable and extensible with both Microsoft.NET and IBM WebSphere and supports the Java 2 Platform, Enterprise Edition (J2EE). So, SAP NetWeaver contains a large set of features and functionalities that support various SAP applications; the R/3 Enterprise System is only one of them. The other applications in the SAP Business Suite include Customer Relationship Management (CRM), Supply Chain Management (SCM), Product Lifecycle Management (PLM), and Business Information Warehouse (BW). SAP NetWeaver is the overall software platform for all of these, and the SAP Web AS is the key system that handles the interactions between the operating system and the application.

With the SAP R/3 System the logical tasks can be run on their own computers. A central computer houses the database, application server computers process the event-driven transactions, and the presentation (client) front-end computers communicate with the application servers. The application servers carry out the actual processing of the dialog transactions, obtaining and updating data from the database and the user. User access is through the graphical user interface (GUI) of the presentation client. The database server processes all data-related requests, such as those of data retrieval and updating the transaction data.

Although a common arrangement is to use a separate computer for each of the presentation, application, and database tiers or layers, the functionality of the SAP Web AS allows these layers to be run on the same computer. That is, the application server and the database server could be run on the same computer, but as separate computer processes on that computer. This is an arrangement that might be used with a small company. On the other hand, for large companies, several application servers and database servers may be utilized to handle their volume of transactions and related data. This capability underscores the scalability of the

SAP R/3 System for use by companies of different size and with varying processing needs.

The SAP R/3 System is designed with an open architecture defined through SAP NetWeaver, which means that it can be run on different computer operating systems, use different database systems, and interface with different desktop systems. It is the SAP Web AS that provides considerable flexibility in the future growth and expansion of the computer hardware and in the arrangement of the logical structure of the R/3 Enterprise System.

Transaction Screens

An SAP R/3 transaction is a series of business-related, logically consistent dialog steps, where each step typically involves a separate screen display for the end user. For these transactions, the graphical presentation of the screen and related processing logic is called a **dynpro** (dynamic program). Each processing module consists of a PBO/PAI module to prepare and process the data displayed or entered on the screen. One screen is processed after the next in a linear sequence as indicated in **Figure 5.2.**

Here, process before output (PBO) is the processing actions that occur before the screen is displayed. This often includes the initialization of the screen fields with default values. Process after input (PAI) is the processing actions that take place when the user clicks the Enter button or otherwise leaves a screen. This often includes processing of any input data or initiating the update to the database. All business transactions do not use the same number of dialog steps. They vary depending on the specified requirements of completing the transaction in the R/3 System. Although PBO and PAI are specific SAP actions, they resemble processing activities that usually occur with other similar screen processing computer applications.

Resource Management

Management of the SAP R/3 System resources is carried out by use of the SAP Web AS. This includes all the tasks involved in the authorization of users of the R/3 System. User authorization can control the transactions and reports that an

FIGURE 5.2
Transaction Dialog Steps

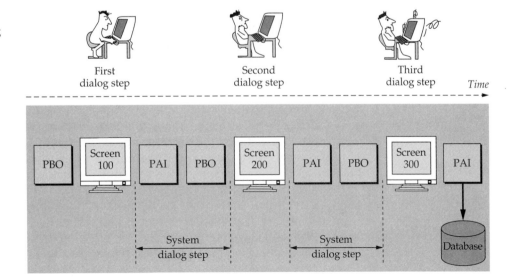

individual user can access and indicate whether the user can view data or enter/change data. The SAP Web AS administration functions are used to specify the distribution of the three-tier client/server resources across the hardware platforms for a particular R/3 System installation.

During the processing of R/3 application module transactions, the **SAP Dispatcher** is a function of the SAP Web AS that runs on an application server as the central control feature, which distributes pending requests to the appropriate defined processes. An application server has the ability to handle the processing of multiple transactions concurrently. The R/3 Dispatcher equally distributes transaction processing within an application server. Each transaction is carried out by a work process, which is run on the application server. A **work process** performs all the actions for dialog processing, updating the database, background (batch) processing, spooling output for printing, and handling lock management (also known as enqueue/dequeue) and the BAPI gateway. **Lock management** ensures that applications do not conflict with one another when accessing data in the R/3 Database. The flexibility of the R/3 System allows a work process to be assigned to any one of the available application servers or to a dedicated application server and is a key aspect of the scalability of the R/3 System. Other activities of the R/3 Dispatcher include managing memory buffer areas, interfacing with the presentation level, and organizing communications activities.

SAP transactions are not necessarily processed by one single R/3 work process; rather, the individual dialog steps of the transaction can be processed by one or more work processes. The R/3 asynchronous update provides the ability to have the dialog part of an SAP transaction and the related database update part of the same transaction handled by different work processes. The work processes can even be carried out on different application server computers. This is accomplished with an SAP **logical unit of work** (LUW). An LUW is capable of handling processing steps that span several actions required to use the database management system software in processing a single SAP transaction. The LUW controls the locks used for the concurrent access and update of the database by more than one user. A Commit Work is used to specify the completion of the steps in a transaction and signals the beginning of the database update processing. An LUW ends with the completion of this update. During the LUW, locks are set as part of the dialog transaction to prevent simultaneous changes to the database. An exclusive mode locks the data to prevent parallel changes. Locked data can only be displayed and processed by a single user. A share mode locks the data so multiple users can display the same data, but only one user can make changes to it.

Lock management is carried out by the enqueue server. This feature protects the applications so they do not conflict with each other when accessing data. The purpose of these locks is to ensure data consistency. A lock remains in effect until a transaction is completed by the update processor. If the user cancels the transaction in the dialog phase or the transaction fails for some other reason, the change request is not issued, and the database update does not take place. Errors during an update may cause the update to terminate without being completed. In this situation any database changes are reversed to maintain database consistency.

The work processes of the SAP Web AS are components that are grouped together in an administrative unit known as an R/3 **Instance.** The services offered by an instance are stopped and started in tandem. An R/3 System administrator or SAP Web AS Consultant establishes the work processes for a particular R/3 application server when the SAP R/3 System is initially installed or reconfigured.

End users do not specify their R/3 Instance. With a distributed R/3 System separate instances can be installed on different computer systems. Processing is then shared across the instances of the R/3 System. The SAP Web AS software encompasses all these features of the SAP R/3 System.

Data Dictionary

A **data dictionary** is a central source of information about an organization's data that contains a description of the data and its significance. It provides the formal attributes of data, such as name, length in characters, and format, and specifies the relationships between the data objects. In the SAP R/3 System this ability is provided by the ABAP Dictionary that is a component of the SAP Web AS software. The ABAP Dictionary stores and manages all data definitions. It ensures the central, nonredundant description of all data used in the R/3 System. All data entered into the ABAP Dictionary is available anywhere in the R/3 System. There is only one Data Dictionary for any given R/3 System installation, whether that system consists of a central instance or of multiple instances. The Data Dictionary is a relational database consisting of many interactive relational tables that include application data and configuration specifications (see **Figure 5.3**).

The Data Dictionary automatically manages all entered and/or changed data, thus ensuring data consistency, data security, and current runtime objects, such as transaction dialog screens. The ABAP programs for processing transactions are stored in this Data Dictionary with the ABAP Dictionary. This ensures that the processing performed is always current at the runtime for a transaction. A **report program** reads and analyzes data in the database tables without changing the database; it displays the result on the screen as a list or prints them. Selection criteria are used to limit the output generated by a report. A **dialog program** allows users to work interactively with the R/3 System so that the contents of the database tables can be changed. The ABAP language and the various features of the Data Dictionary are provided by the SAP Web AS software.

FIGURE 5.3
Data Dictionary
Integration

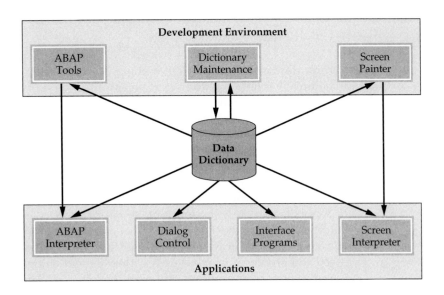

Object Migration

A recommended technical configuration of an SAP R/3 System implementation consists of three separate systems that are used to support distinct phases of development and production activities. A **development** system (or instance) is used for the configuration of the SAP R/3 application modules where user data, which is entered by a configuration specialist, specifies the processes of the best business practices that have been selected for implementation. A **quality assurance** (QA) testing system is used to isolate the development phase from final testing and the user training environment from final production. A **production** system (or instance) consists of the live business transactions and company data of the final configuration. Under this arrangement, each system is a separate instance with its own data. This system organization facilitates the addition or revision of business processes in a safe manner that does not affect the production environment until any changes have been completed, thoroughly tested, and the users have been trained. R/3 application modules are developed and tested without interfering with the production system. For R/3 System upgrades, modifications are made in the development system and then automatically transported to the production system. Under this migration process the daily workflow of an organization is not disrupted by new development activities.

The corrections and transport feature of the SAP Web AS supports the phased implementation by providing the mechanism for moving or migrating objects from one system to another. The **corrections** operation audits R/3 object modifications to carry out version management that tracks current and obsolete versions of an object, such as a dialog transaction screen. The **transport** feature moves the object from one system to another, such as from development to QA testing. The original source for an object can only exist in one system, the development system. Copies of the object are then migrated to the QA testing and to the production systems. Version management tracks the changes to objects so that when future modifications are made, only the modified changes are copied to the target system using the transport utility. This tracking is a built-in feature included as a component of the SAP Web AS software.

Electronic Data Interchange

Electronic data interchange (EDI) is one of several SAP R/3 System communication features that help provide the seamless integration of software and technology for moving data between one R/3 System and another R/3 or non-R/3 System. **EDI** provides an electronic means for business partners to communicate and to transact business by using standard communication protocols in the support of supply chain management. This facilitates the automated exchange of data between the SAP R/3 System and the application systems of a business partner. The partner may be another SAP R/3 System or any other computer system. A key aspect of EDI is the movement of data from one business application to another. This is more than merely sending a file of information from one computer system to the other. With EDI the data comes out of one application system and is received by the other application system, such as data from a purchase order system being received and processed by a business partner's order entry system.

EDI messages may be either outbound or inbound. An outbound message is one that is sent from the SAP R/3 System to another system, while an inbound message is one that is received from another system. The R/3 System contains software modules that generate EDI outbound messages via an **intermediate document** (IDOC) interface. The processing of inbound EDI messages is also based on IDOCs with an open standardized interface that supports real-time EDI processing.

The main component of the EDI interface is the IDOC. An **IDOC** is an SAP data transfer container for the exchange of data between SAP Systems or between SAP Systems and external systems. The IDOCs conform to an SAP R/3 standard that determines the structure and format of the data for electronic transmission. IDOCs trigger a functional set of application transactions for processing the business transaction. IDOCs are independent of the business partner and are identical for inbound and outbound processing.

The EDI architecture provided by the SAP Web AS consists of three primary elements. An EDI-enabled application is an R/3 application that supports the automatic processing of business transactions received from external business partners. An EDI interface consists of temporary structures (IDOCs) and the function modules or programs that connect the interface to the application. From inbound messages an EDI subsystem converts the IDOCs to EDI messages from the external business partner system and reverses the processing for outbound messages. SAP does not provide this element of the EDI architecture; however, a number of suitable converters are available from third-party vendors for different EDI messages. In this manner the SAP Web AS supports the EDI technical architecture for processing EDI transactions between the application systems of business partners for end-to-end extended supply chain management.

Application Link Enabling

Application Link Enabling (ALE) is a message-based architecture that enables the integration of loosely coupled SAP R/3 applications. Technical, organizational, and economic reasons often require that SAP R/3 System applications are separated. For example, a production plant may be located far from the main office of an organization. In this situation the best R/3 System arrangement may be to install and operate application components locally—and as a technically independent separate instance. This would permit the assignment of business functions, such as inventory management or central purchasing, to organizational units that are separate R/3 installations. However, certain business functions require direct access to data in another R/3 System, such as a distribution center accessing the finished product. Examples of distributed SAP R/3 business processes are (1) central financial system with local logistics systems, (2) local processing of customer orders and central shipping functions, and (3) independent, local warehouse management systems and central logistics. ALE supports the structuring and operating of distributed R/3 applications. The R/3 applications run independently with their own separate data in the distributed applications. The integration of the R/3 applications is not accomplished using a central database, but rather by using synchronous and asynchronous communication. Synchronous data transfer occurs between ABAP programs via remote function call (RFC) communications. This requires a connection between the two R/3 Systems while a transaction is being processed. Asynchronous data transfer allows the sender and receiver R/3 System to operate independently of each other. The data to be transferred is stored to a temporary file and transfers the data to the receiving R/3 System at a scheduled time.

For ALE, the foundation of data exchange is the IDOC that follows similar processing with the EDI interface. The IDOC type determines the SAP processing module that receives the IDOC for inbound processing. During processing, an IDOC is transferred to the ALE layer, where it is formatted for sending and then communicated to the receiving SAP System. After the transmission is complete, the IDOC is imported into the target system, where it initiates inbound processing.

Data that is transferred using ALE includes transaction data, master data, and control and customization data. Subsets or views of the master data that represent changes are usually transferred to reduce the volume of data transmitted. Customization data that is transferred includes business organization data such as the definition of company codes, plants, and purchasing organizations. During the installation of an SAP R/3 System, the arrangement of the distributed systems is determined, the applications run on each system are defined, and the transport of the transaction data and the relevant master and control data are specified. The features of ALE are a component of the SAP Web AS software that supports all of the SAP R/3 application modules.

Workflow Environment

A **workflow management system** provides the procedures for automating business processes. It coordinates the sequence of steps and the activities of the users involved, and it provides the software functions necessary for processing business transactions. SAP Business Workflow is incorporated at an integration level "above" the transaction level and uses the existing R/3 transactions and function modules. The existing functions and operability of the transactions and function modules are neither changed nor restricted by the workflow control. As an example of workflow, consider the handling of customer inquiries and orders. These pass through several departments, and different users add data at different steps in the processing. Data entered by one user is passed to the next users in the processing sequence. A workflow established in the R/3 System handles this passing of data for processing the transaction by the next user and notifies the user that the transaction data is available for continued processing. Another example is the approval of travel expenses. A user completes a travel expense transaction. Once completed, that data is passed to a supervisor for approval. This may continue for several levels of approval. The workflow for the travel expense transaction would define this passing of data to the next user (supervisor) for the approval. In this manner SAP Business Workflow provides procedural automation of business processes by managing the sequence of work activities and the invocation of appropriate human and/or computer resources with the various activity steps.

The SAP Business Workflow Management links data with business routines and makes sure that it is transferred to the staff member designated as the next individual to handle the processing of the transaction. The appropriate staff member receives transaction-related messages in his or her electronic inbox that are automatically processed by the SAP R/3 System. For those events that require human intervention, the staff members designated with the authority to continue the processing of the transaction need to respond only to the transactions delivered in their electronic inboxes.

Workflow integration exists at a level that is above the transaction level, because it needs to support the automation of routine tasks for an entire business process across individual R/3 transactions. This transcendent workflow integration supports users in managing their daily work and ensures the execution of all work items using notification and alert techniques.

The technical components of SAP Business Workflow include the definition tools and the runtime environment. The definition tools describe the links among the processes and people related to processing a complete business transaction. The runtime environment controls the operation of the workflow through the various steps for completion. The processing of workflow is a feature provided within the SAP Web AS software.

Remote Function Call

A remote function call (RFC) is the protocol for internal and external calls to special subprograms known as function modules. These are managed in their own function library in the R/3 System. The difference between an internal call and one across computer boundaries is merely a special destination parameter that specifies the target computer that is to process the program. RFC communication is bi-directional; ABAP programs can call external services, and external applications can call R/3 services. RFCs simplify the programming of communication processes between computer systems that support both synchronous and asynchronous communication. The technical requirements for RFCs correspond to those for business application program interfaces (BAPIs). A BAPI is a method applied to an SAP business object that performs a specific business task. BAPIs are stored in the R/3 System as RFC-enabled function modules within the ABAP Workbench.

RFCs are the foundation for providing object linking and embedding (OLE) to desktop applications such as Microsoft Word, Excel, and Access. This facilitates the direct communication and exchange of data with an SAP R/3 System. RFCs are a feature of the SAP Web AS to support these activities for transferring data among internal and external applications.

Quick Check

1. List the three main task areas of the SAP R/3 System that provide for a distributed processing environment.

2. True or false: An instance is an administrative unit in which components of an R/3 System are grouped together to provide one or more services that are started and stopped in tandem.

3. Dialog processing and lock management are both examples of a _____ process in the R/3 System.

4. The _____ ensures the central, nonredundant description of data used in an R/3 System.

5. True or false: The Correction and Transport utilities in the R/3 System are used to manage the user data in the database.

6. True or false: ALE is a message-based architecture that enables the integration of tightly coupled applications.

7. _____ allows the integration of Windows application programs with R/3 applications.

Chapter 6

Internet-Enabled Solutions

Internet Platform

The **Internet platform** is the computer architecture that supports using Internet technology to conduct business on the Internet. The Internet provides a standard platform for all kinds of data exchange between individuals and organizations. This data exchange includes both the external Internet connectivity and the internal intranets used within a business by its employees. Using this Internet technology, companies are evolving toward a communication-centered model. The Internet allows business processes to be extended beyond the boundaries of an enterprise by using an extended supply chain that integrates a business's processes with those of its vendors and customers. Company information is now available to customers, end consumers, and business partners. Businesses can take advantage of the rich functionality of the SAP R/3 Enterprise System combined with the attractive and easy-to-use format of the Internet platform. With an intranet, a business can use Internet technology to enable its own employees to carry out R/3 transactions from their web browser, without the need to have the proprietary SAPGUI client installed on their workstation computers. This includes **employee self-service,** in which all employees in an organization can access their human resource records and maintain those records directly, such as changing their address. The Internet platform leverages the features of worldwide, around-the-clock availability with the intuitive, easy-to-use web browser interface. Use of the Internet minimizes different end-user interfaces and maintenance requirements while delivering business applications in a portable environment. Because of its open architecture design, the R/3 System can readily accommodate business processes that use the Internet platform.

To effectively conduct commerce via the Internet requires not just communication, but enterprise business application software. The R/3 System is suited for business on the Internet. Its three-tier architecture uses a lean client that requires only a personal computer as an end-user workstation. Internet applications are designed to be used by a much larger audience than other business applications that use proprietary interfaces, such as the SAPGUI. Internet applications must be simple and easy to use, even for occasional users. The Internet platform is well suited for replacing the proprietary SAPGUI client with an Internet web browser client on an end user's workstation.

Classifying Internet Applications

Internet applications are frequently classified as consumer-to-business and business-to-business relationships. In a **consumer-to-business** (C2B) relationship, the consumer uses a web browser to access the vendor's business system to review a product catalog, place an order, or inquire about a product or service. C2B applications benefit from offering products and services to consumers all over the world. Consumers benefit from the ease of navigation on the Internet. They can establish a real-time connection to the business system, which provides immediate feedback for consumer decision making. Consumers have immediate access to a continually expanding range of products offered by a business.

In **business-to-business** (B2B) relationships, integrated business systems can cooperate with each other directly for extended supply chain management. Information regarding order numbers, customers, and invoices can be exchanged. This enables an electronic marketplace that facilitates ad hoc B2B matching and synchronization of purchase requisitions and sales orders from independent R/3 Systems through a common transaction. B2B relationships involve an Internet connection that provides communication directly with the core business transaction applications of the business partners. This business application–to–business application interaction is much more than just having an employee use a web browser to access an Internet web server of the business partner. It is the connection through the web server into the transaction processing application of the trading partner.

API interfaces support B2B Web-based connectivity. An API (**application program interface**) is an interface that is used by one application program to communicate with the application programs of other systems. APIs provide the interface technology that allows Web pages to be created more easily from SAP R/3 transactions and that facilitates B2B Web interactions.

Intranet applications, which use Internet technology for communication within a single enterprise, support a class of SAP R/3 users who can access the R/3 System using only their web browser, rather than using the proprietary SAPGUI. These employees are likely to be more casual users of the R/3 System transactions. With these occasional users, the web browser becomes a preferred user interface. The Internet platform increases the feasibility of moving data entry from a specialized operation within a business to the point at which the data actually originates.

Web-Enabled Transactions

Web-enabled SAP R/3 transactions can be used for many of the R/3 application modules. These include sales and distribution (SD), materials management (MM), production planning (PP), quality management (QM), financial (FI), and human resources (HR). In sales and distribution (SD) these transactions include a product catalog or product variant configuration. The product catalog is used for pricing, availability checking, purchase requisitions, and order entry. Variant configuration allows a customer to specify how a product is configured. For example, in placing an order for a computer, the type of processor, amount of memory, size of monitor, and other features are specified. The resulting configuration is tested for consistency, and an order is created that is posted to production. This reduces lead time and provides more efficient customer service. For material management (MM), requisitions and stock requests are transactions that can be Web enabled. The quantity, material, plant, and delivery date are readily entered when creating the requisition. A search by product group or material class can be done to help locate the desired product.

Stock requests handle both incoming and outgoing transfers from inventory. This can be for work-in-process inventories, consignment stocks, or other inventory processing. In production planning (PP), Kanban and availability inquiries are readily handled via the Internet. **Kanban** is a Japanese term that identifies a method of replenishing materials in a production/inventory environment. Suppliers use their web browsers to access a customer's Kanban board and view the Kanbans for which they are responsible. They replenish an empty Kanban by creating a shipment in their own system that results in the delivery of the necessary products to the customer. With this extended supply chain the business processes are outside the boundaries of the company, and the responsibility for shipment is transferred from the manufacturer to the supplier. With **available to promise** (ATP), a customer uses a web browser to connect to a supplier's R/3 System to inquire about a material, plant, quantity, and planned delivery date. If the conditions are met, then a delivery date is quoted. Customers get the information for themselves, in real time, and improve their ordering process. Plant maintenance (PM) involves the recording of various measurement readings concerning equipment wear and usage. Measurement readings describe a condition at a measuring point at a particular moment, such as the speed in revolutions per minute of the rotor shaft of a wind turbine power generator. These observed readings can be entered manually by use of a web browser, or an Internet connection can be used to transmit the readings at scheduled times. Inspection results and other quality data can be delivered from the quality management (QM) application to customers for their use.

With Internet access, customers in the automotive, chemical, and pharmaceutical industries can get a certificate of analysis where and when they need it, so that the certificate does not need to be created and shipped with the product. For the financial (FI) application, payment requests and reminder notices can be sent via the Internet to expedite processing. Ad hoc financial reports and standard executive information systems reports can be produced for access, on demand, via an executive's web browser. The Internet enables employee self-service for the human resources (HR) applications. Job openings can be posted and job applications received over the Internet. Companies receive the information they need directly in a format that makes it easier to process applications. Applicants can trace the status of their applications at any time by using a unique identifier to access their information. This provides a smoother, friendlier employment application process.

Business-to-Business Application Communication

SAP R/3 is an open system in which business process applications are accessible via defined and standardized interfaces. A business application programming interface (BAPI) is a well-defined interface for accessing the processes and data of a business application system. BAPIs facilitate the communication of different applications of various companies via the Internet. One BAPI can extract data from an R/3 System and transmit it via the Internet to another R/3 System where another BAPI processes the incoming data. Or, it could be transmitted to a non-SAP R/3 System where a different BAPI can be used to transfer the data to the other business application. For example, one company's purchase order can be sent directly to and processed by another company's order-entry system without human intervention by the order-entry clerk or without a predefined point-to-point EDI transaction. BAPIs created in cooperation with SAP customers,

Microsoft, and standards organizations provide these robust R/3 System Internet components that leverage the R/3 functionality and furnish long-term stable interfaces to the R/3 System.

Internet Transaction Server

The uncoupling of business rules from the database and the openness for graphical interfaces make it easy for the three-tier architecture of the R/3 System to be extended to a multitier R/3 Internet architecture that ensures scalability, multitasking, and performance, even with high volumes of data. The classic three-tier R/3 System architecture with its "thin" client supports the lower-bandwidth restrictions of the Internet. Without the need to replace or re-create business processes, corporations can use their existing three-tier architecture that is readily extended to a multitier structure with the additional components that provide the Internet support that makes a web browser the R/3 client (see **Figure 6.1**). To

FIGURE 6.1 **R/3 Multitier Architecture**

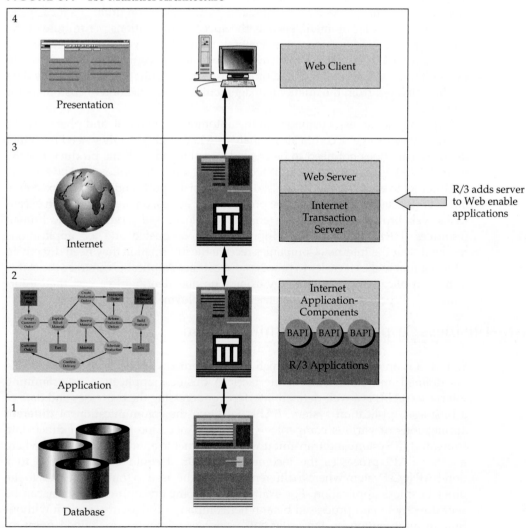

accomplish this, the multitier architecture introduces an additional Internet layer that is between the existing application layer and the web browser client layer. When the web browser is used as the R/3 client, the client becomes even thinner. The benefits to corporations include a single point of control for all software maintenance and upgrades.

Internet Web pages mirror SAP R/3 transactions (see **Figure 6.2**). The HTML Web pages delivered to the end user's web browser mirror the transaction screens of the R/3 System displayed using the SAPGUI. Users familiar with the proprietary SAPGUI easily recognize the overall structure of the Web page.

The **Internet transaction server** (ITS) is a gateway between the Hypertext Transfer Protocol (HTTP) of the Web page and the SAPGUI protocol from the R/3 application server (see **Figure 6.3**). The SAP Integrated ITS is part of the SAP Web Application Server. Basically, screens processed in the application server as part of an SAP transaction are mapped to the Hypertext Markup Language (HTML) for the Web pages transmitted via the Internet to a user's web browser for display. The context of an R/3 Internet transaction represents the data that is passed between the application server and the web browser. The ITS uses this context to produce

FIGURE 6.2
From R/3 Screen to Web Page

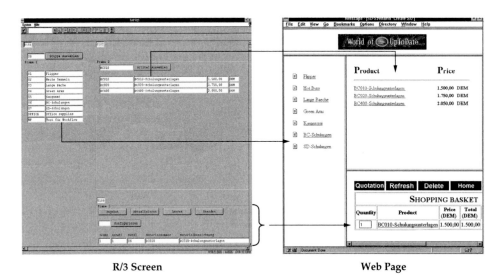

R/3 Screen   Web Page

FIGURE 6.3
Conversion Process from R/3 Screen to Web Page

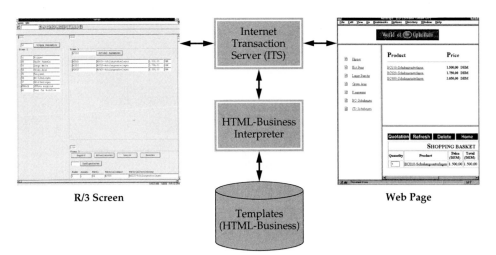

R/3 Screen   Web Page

the HTML for the web browser and to interpret a response from the web browser for processing by the application server. HTML templates are used by the ITS as a description of how the field and table data are to be merged to create the HTML document sent to the web browser. HTML-Business is a structured programming language developed by SAP AG to specify how R/3 data and variables are to be merged with HTML for the web browser.

The SAP Web Basis is the architecture that processes the Internet-enabled trans-actions. As illustrated in **Figure 6.4,** when a request is received by the Web Host from the Client web browser, the Web Host starts the ITS. The ITS reads the ser-vice description and starts the transaction on the R/3 Application Server. R/3 processes the transaction in the same manner it would process a transaction from the proprietary SAPGUI client. The ITS generates an HTML page using R/3 trans-action data and an HTML-Business template. The resulting HTML page is sent from the ITS to the Web Host, which is the web server that sends the HTML to the web browser for display and action by the end user.

Recent developments of NetWeaver have incorporated the ITS into the SAP Web Application Server as the Integrated ITS. As a result, the Integrated ITS is installed automatically with the SAP Web AS. No separate installation is needed. However, to support the upward compatibility of R/3 System releases, a Standalone ITS can be used as may be needed. The Standalone ITS and the SAP Web AS coexist with the Integrated ITS (**Figure 6.5**). Eventually Web AS will move exclusively to the

FIGURE 6.4
SAP Web
Processing
Architecture

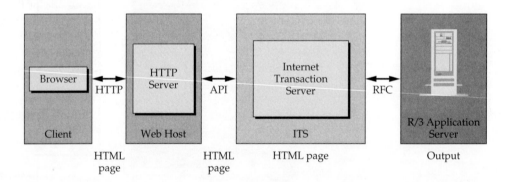

FIGURE 6.5
Coexistence of
Standalone ITS and
SAP Web AS
Integrated ITS

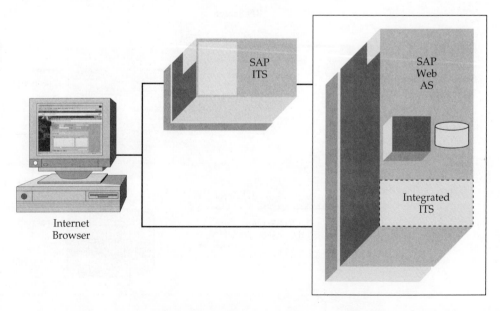

Integrated ITS. This will ensure better flow of a transaction through the SAP Web AS to either an Internet browser or the SAPGUI.

Approaches to Web-Enabled Transactions

There are two approaches to Web-enabled R/3 transactions (**Figure 6.6**). The **Inside-Out approach** uses the ITS with the Web application component inside the R/3 System. The **Outside-In approach** consists of all other processes for Web enabling the R/3 System and is also known as the "Rest of the World" approach. Here, the Web application component is outside the R/3 System and is typically developed using Visual Basic, C, or Java.

With the Inside-Out approach, each Web page is one screen that would have been produced for the SAPGUI client. Programming in this approach is completely supported within the SAP development environment. The Internet Communication Manager delivers the HTTP or other format Web pages. Standard components are upgraded as part of the normal SAP upgrade process. For the Outside-In approach, each Web page is often more than one screen for the SAPGUI client. A broad spectrum of development environments is external to the SAP development environment. Upgrades to the R/3 System that affect the Web pages require that separate changes are made to those pages. While the ITS provides for secure access from the Internet to all SAP transactions, the Outside-In approach requires the application of transactional integrity outside of the R/3 environment. The Inside-Out approach to R/3 transaction is delivered through mySAP.com Workplace. This is a recent functionality of the R/3 System that Web enables R/3 transactions in a more user-friendly way, with components for several previous R/3 screens combined in a visually appealing and ergonomically functional layout in a single pane of a Web page. The mySAP.com Workplace turns the R/3 web browser into a desktop for both R/3 and non-R/3 applications. This Web enabling of the R/3 System increases its ease of use and access for both frequent and casual R/3 System users and leverages the use of the Internet platform in delivering business process information to the desktop.

FIGURE 6.6
Approaches to Web-Enabled R/3 Systems

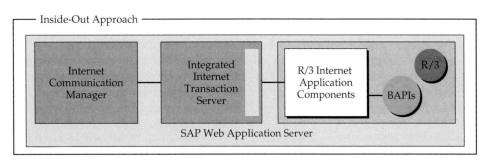

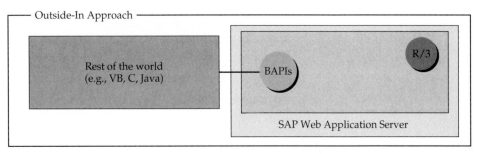

Quick Check

1. True or false: A Web-enabled enterprise software application reduces its availability.

2. List the three classifications of Internet applications.

3. Internet applications must be simple and require little or no _____ to use.

4. A Web page from R/3 _____ its corresponding transaction from the application server.

5. Job applications and "who is who" are two Web-enabled applications of the _____ application module.

6. True or false: A BAPI is used in separating business logic from user interfaces to create an "open system."

7. True or false: The SAP Internet Transaction Server is a gateway between the R/3 transaction and the HTML Web document.

Chapter 7

Configuration

What Is Configuration?

The R/3 Enterprise System is a **table-driven application.** That is, it makes extensive use of relatively static data stored in a file or database table and is used in controlling processing within the application software. A simple example of "table-driven" is an income tax table used to determine the appropriate tax rate used in payroll processing. Any changes to the tax rates are made to the externally stored table, and not to the internal program code itself. Another example is an *.INI file; such files are used frequently with operating systems software and desktop software. A somewhat more complex example is that of a rollup table, which is used regularly in the consolidation of business unit application data. A **rollup table** specifies the relationship among business units in an organization hierarchy. An organization structure is stored externally to the program code as a relatively static or persistent specification. Changes to an organization structure are made by revising the table entries. Table-driven design greatly enhances the flexibility of an application by storing relatively persistent data external to the program code and is used in most purchased software, including enterprise software, such as the SAP R/3 Enterprise System.

Configuration is the means by which user selections and relatively static data are specified for the R/3 System. This **customizing data** is stored in database tables in the SAP repository. (See **Figure 7.1.**) This includes the specification of the persistent, customizing data that delineates an organization structure and a chart of accounts—that is, the persistent data for table-driven software. Configuration also includes the selection of the processes themselves that will be used in its implementation. Additionally, the details of the configuration may include the available fields displayed on an interactive screen. The R/3 System makes extensive use of table-driven design, with database tables holding the persistent configuration specifications that constitute the customizing data.

In the configuration procedures the available SAP business process procedures (BPPs) are selected and matched with a company's business requirements and workflow processes. That is, a company's transaction processing requirements are mapped to the available BPPs in the R/3 System (see **Figure 7.2**). This matching and mapping is **business process reengineering** (BPR), in which the existing business processes of an organization are changed, revised, and adopted to match up with the best business practice processes available in the R/3 System. Most of the effort of configuration is in determining the functions to be implemented and the values for specifying the relatively static parameters used by the R/3 System

FIGURE 7.1
Repository
Contains
Configuration
Settings

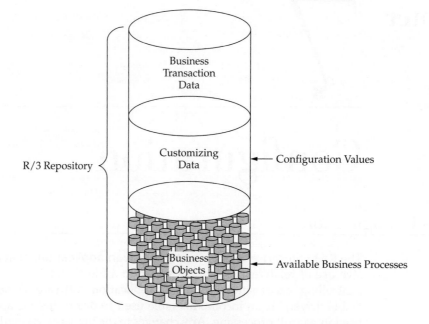

FIGURE 7.2
Configuration
Maps Business
Requirements to
SAP R/3 System

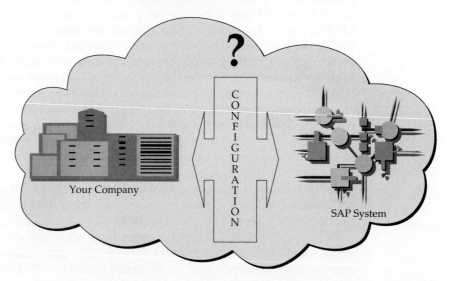

in its table-driven processes. Clearly, actually entering those values in the R/3 System becomes a nearly mechanical task, once their values have been determined. To configure an R/3 System installation, the implementation team must:

- Understand the business processes or functions available in the R/3 System
- Understand the business requirements of the business in which the R/3 System is being installed
- Know how to use the R/3 System configuration tools that are available to do the actual implementation entries

The challenge for someone new to SAP R/3 Enterprise is to learn about both the SAP business process functions and the SAP configuration tools before participating in an R/3 System installation. One way to begin learning about the available

SAP business functions and transactions is to learn the processing that can be performed in the application modules such as finance and human resources. This usually involves learning how transactions are processed using the IDES training data available from SAP AG. For example, learning the available transactions in human resources is a first step in learning the business processing functions that can be performed using that application module. Part II of this book provides you with a start in learning about some of these available transactions.

Many configuration activities are conducted using the SAP Solution Manager. **Solution Manager** is a set of tools and functions that help manage software solutions throughout their entire life cycle: from initial implementation through operations and continuous improvement. It runs in a separate central system or instance using the SAP Web Application Server platform to which other SAP systems are connected. With Solution Manager, configuration is performed by selecting business process procedures (BPPs) from the Repository (see **Figure 7.3**). Where a need exists for additional functionality, especially in the reporting requirements, customer-created processes are included in the Repository and used in the configuration.

Configuration is the primary activity for every SAP R/3 project, whether it is an initial installation or a subsequent process change or upgrade. Configuration is frequently accomplished by using **Accelerated SAP** (ASAP), which is a computer systems analysis and design method, and by using tools provided by SAP AG. Solution Manager is the SAP platform by which the ASAP methodology and tool set are used in configuration. Solution Manager is a new platform that provides better integration of the previously developed ASAP tool set. Thus, Solution Manager deploys the following: ASAP methodology for implementing and continually optimizing the system (see ASAP Roadmap, **Figure 7.4**), a means for selecting business processes (SAP Reference Structure), a graphical description of business processes (R/3 Reference Structure in Diagram Explorer), menu-led parameter settings (Implementation Guide or IMG), project management tools that operate

FIGURE 7.3
Configuration Selects Business Process from the Repository

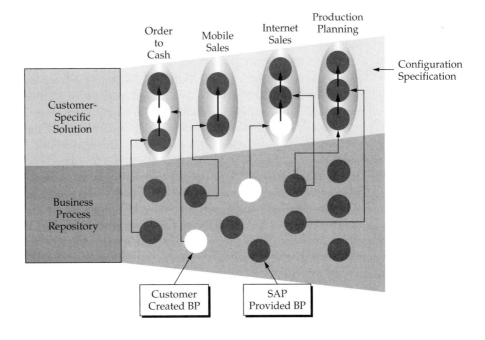

FIGURE 7.4
ASAP Roadmap
and Solution
Manager Drive
Configuration of
SAP Products

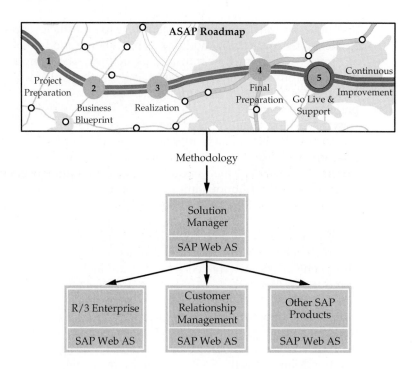

with Microsoft Project, and a model company (IDES) in a training database that is fully integrated and preconfigured for use in training and testing. In **Figure 7.4** notice that each of these SAP products makes use of the same SAP Web Application Server that is a key component of NetWeaver.

The Reference Structure for a typical business is selected and specified as part of the R/3 System software installation. This is then configured by changing parameter settings to meet the particular requirements of the company that will use R/3 for its business transactions. It is this configuration that involves mapping an organization's requirements to SAP's available business functions and selecting the appropriate BPPs.

The ASAP Roadmap provides a framework for carrying out an R/3 System implementation using Solution Manager. Its primary purpose is to manage the customization process to ensure that all the required activities have been completed for a successful implementation. This framework structures the implementation process as phases, work packages, and project task activities. ASAP is a repeatable method that can be used with different implementations of R/3 and provides a standard approach to SAP implementation projects. This is of particular importance to SAP AG and other consultants who assist in the configuration of R/3 Systems in many different organizations. Solution Manager provides the consultants a standard "playbook" for doing an R/3 System implementation.

Reference Structure

Companies need tools to help them quickly recognize the integrated functionality and scope of the SAP R/3 System and to evaluate its usability for their company's situation. The Reference Structure is used to identify, document, and represent existing enterprise business processes in the R/3 System. The Reference Structure provides guidance in answering questions such as:

- How can a company identify and document existing business processes?
- Which functions and integration options does the R/3 System offer?
- How can a company define the interfaces between the R/3 System and other systems?
- How can a company optimize its business processes with the R/3 System?

The R/3 Reference Structure, which is used within ASAP, helps companies quickly identify required business processes. It facilitates requirements and gap analysis. In performing **gap analysis,** the business processes necessary to satisfy a company's transaction processing requirements are compared with the functionality of the processes provided by the R/3 System applications to determine the potential gaps between the R/3 System and these requirements. These gaps are then addressed to complete the implementation. Alternative solutions can be explored so the gaps are removed by matching appropriate R/3 System business processes with the company's requirements.

The R/3 Reference Structure contains all the common business process procedures (BPPs), linked in a totally integrated fashion that can be deployed by a company without further adjustment. However, the standard R/3 Reference Structure usually includes many functions and data structures that are not relevant to a particular company. The process of configuration is where the system implementation team adjusts the R/3 Reference Structure until it fits the needs of the specific company. This is how BPR is carried out within the R/3 Enterprise System. When the configuration activities have matched the business requirements to the processing available in the Reference Structure, the completed model is known as an **Enterprise Data Model.**

The R/3 Reference Structure in Solution Manager supports the analysis of the R/3 Application System: the business processes, functions, and events together with the organizational elements. Through this analysis the business processes, functions, events, data, and organizational elements are specified to configure the R/3 System to meet the requirements of a particular company. The Reference Structure is used with the ASAP methodology to provide a consistent procedure for implementing an R/3 System within an organization. Also, the Reference Structure is useful in training, where it can provide an understanding of the available business functions that is needed in matching R/3 functionality with business requirements.

The **SAP Reference IMG** within Solution Manager is an integral part of the R/3 System that is used extensively in the configuration of the R/3 System. This Reference IMG in Solution Manager is the same as that in the R/3 Enterprise System, because they both run on top of the SAP Web Application Server of NetWeaver. These IMGs are used to access and work with the customizing settings of the Reference Structure. The menu selections for opening the SAP Reference IMG are as follows:

Select **Tools** → **Customizing** → **IMG** → **Edit Project**

The Customizing: Execute Project screen appears for continuing selections.

Click the **SAP Reference IMG** button on the Application toolbar.

The **Display IMG** screen (see **Figure 7.5**) displays a list of the business application components that are available for the current release of the SAP R/3 System

FIGURE 7.5
Available
Application
Components in
IMG

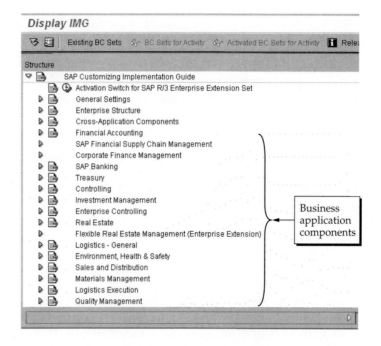

and are consequently included in the R/3 Reference Structure. In general, these encompass the application modules introduced previously in Chapter 1. Because of the important role of the IMG in configuration, you will examine it in additional detail in this chapter and in subsequent chapters of this book.

System Landscape

The **system landscape** contains all the SAP Systems that are installed for an organization. It often consists of several systems whose SAP Systems are linked by transport routes. SAP AG recommends a three-system landscape in which each of the central clients has its own SAP System (see **Figure 7.6**) and as a result is installed on a separate instance of the SAP Web AS. The three-system landscape consists of a development system (DEV), a quality assurance system (QAS), and a production system (PRD). The production system is where an organization actually uses the R/3 System in carrying out its day-to-day business operations. This is where the real, live transaction data exists for the organization. DEV and QAS are R/3 System instances that provide support to the PRD system. All configuration activities with the various entries and changes to Customization data and Repository objects occur in the Customizing client (CUST) of the DEV system. When CUST is ready, that client is released with its change requests. The CUST client is transported, using the **Change and Transport System** (CTS), into the quality assurance client in the QAS system. The QAS system is used to ensure changes have been transported with tests conducted to confirm the transports are complete. If the tests in QAS are successful, the change requests are finally transported into the PRD system. As a common practice, other clients are set up in the DEV and QAS system instances. In DEV, clients are used for development testing (TEST), for prototyping (SAND), and for developing customer processes (DVLP). In QAS a client is also used for training. During these configuration activities some of the

FIGURE 7.6
Three-System
Landscape of
Configuration

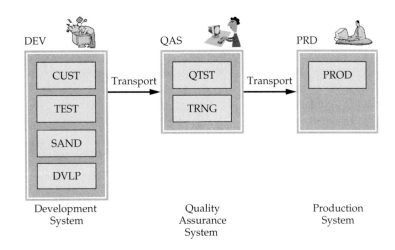

customizing data is cross-client data and applies to all the clients in that instance. Cross-client data is included in the transport from DEV to QAS. This three-system landscape is of most importance to configuring an R/3 System, because the landscape is the environment where the customization activities of configuration are actually performed, tested, and ultimately placed into production.

The "Big Picture"

The purpose of the "Big Picture" is to show the primary interactions among the Implementation Roadmap, the Solution Manager, and the DEV instance (see **Figure 7.7**). The Implementation Roadmap is the overall framework carrying out the configuration. This framework drives the use of the tool set for the ASAP methodology in the Solution Manager. A Business Blueprint is created consisting of selected business processes that satisfy an organization's requirements. They are delineated as specific Phases, Work Packages, Activities, and Tasks for the configuration. The configuration activities take place in the DEV instance of the three-system landscape. Here the CUST client is where the customization settings are performed that do the configuration in the IMG. About 80 percent of a typical R/3 System installation is handled by the IMG configuration setting. Another 10 percent are enhancements, while 10 percent are customer developed. During an R/3 System installation no modification should be made to the SAP Web AS or to the BPPs that are provided with the R/3 System. As the configuration process unfolds for an installation, transport using CTS moves the configuration to the QAS and PROD systems of the three-system landscape.

Business Object Repository

The **Business Object Repository** (BOR) is the central depository for the SAP business process procedures (BPPs) that make up the R/3 System. The BOR provides an object-oriented view of all processes and data in the R/3 System. These repository objects are the fundamental elements at the atomic or lowest level in the R/3 System. In the configuration process the specification and selection of BPPs is carried out to activate those processes necessary to meet business requirements.

FIGURE 7.7
The "Big Picture" of
Configuration

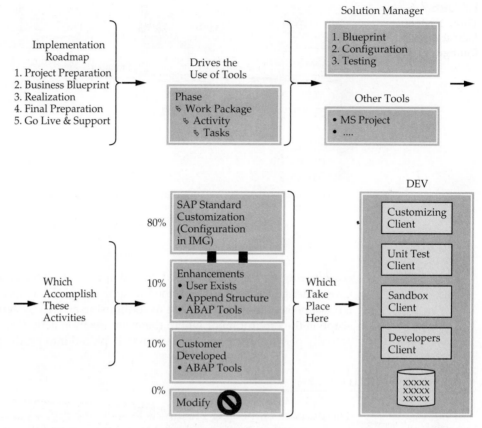

FIGURE 7.8
Access to Business
Object Repository

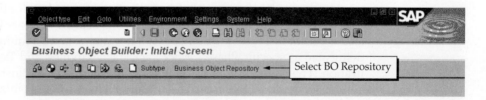

The objects are arranged according to the component hierarchy illustrated in the IMG as shown previously in **Figure 7.5.**

You can access BPP objects in the BOR. This is accomplished with the Business Object Builder (Transaction SWO1). The menu selections for opening the application component hierarchy in the BOR are as follows:

Select **Tools** → **ABAP Workbench** → **Development** → **Business Object Builder**

The Business Object Builder: Initial Screen appears for continuing selections. (See **Figure 7.8.**)

Click the **Business Object Repository** button on the Application toolbar. The Business Object Repository Browser: Entry Screen displays as a dialog box. Next click the **Business Objects / Organization Types** option button. Then click the **Continue (Enter)** button. The Application Components hierarchy displays (see **Figure 7.9**). Notice the similarity between the components in **Figure 7.9** and those

FIGURE 7.9
Application
Components in
Business Object
Repository

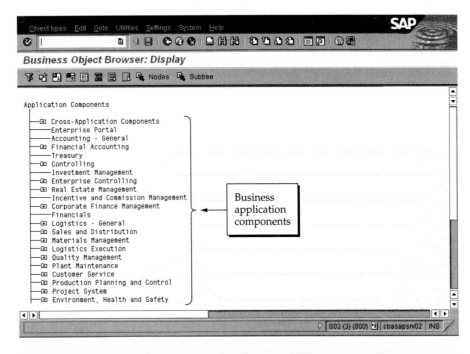

FIGURE 7.10
Process Selection
Matrix

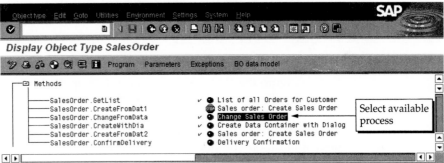

of the IMG in **Figure 7.5,** although some components at this level have slightly different names. Clearly, the IMG facilitates the configuration of the atomic-level BPPs.

You can now forward reference (drill down) to a specific business object. Expand **Sales and Distribution;** expand **Methods.** A list of available methods displays, which represents business processes at the atomic level. (See **Figure 7.10.**)

Now, double-click **Change Sales Order.** The BAPI_SALESORDER_CHANGE displays, and its source code and interface are available for your review. (See **Figure 7.11.**)

As you can see from **Figure 7.11,** this is not exactly the end user–friendly method for examining business objects and for selecting those that implement the desired best business practices in an organization. Solution Manager and the IMG provide considerably more friendly methods of selecting BPPs. Solution Manager with the ASAP methodology furnishes the most friendly approach based on business requirements. The IMG provides for more direct selection when you have considerable knowledge of the R/3 System and know the particular BPPs that are to be implemented during configuration. So the need for and role of the Solution Manager in configuration are clear.

FIGURE 7.11
Example Business Process Code for SALESORDER_CHANGE Object

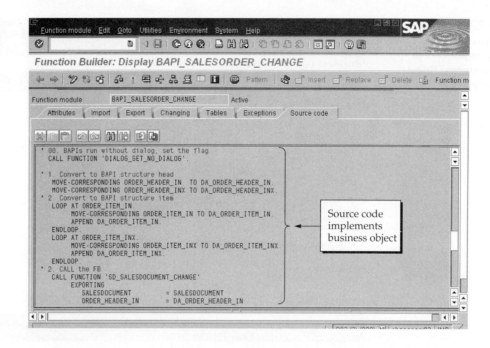

Implementation Guide

The **Implementation Guide** (IMG) is an R/3 System tool for making the settings that configure the R/3 System to meet a company's requirements. It supports a detailed, online method designed to help configure the R/3 System efficiently and rapidly. The IMG provides detailed menus for configuring and setting the application modules. The SAP **Reference IMG** contains documentation on all the business application components supplied by SAP AG, as illustrated previously in **Figure 7.5.** A **Project IMG** is a subset of the Reference IMG that contains the documentation for selected IMG components that are implemented as part of a specific configuration project. By creating a special Project IMG view, such as "mandatory activities," you can reduce the number of implementation activities to what is relevant for a specific configuration undertaking. Once a related group of configuration settings is completed, the Customizing Management System (CMS) is used with the SAP Transport System to export those configuration settings to other R/3 Systems or to other clients within the same R/3 System.

A key activity completed early in the configuration process is the establishment of the enterprise structure, which determines the selection and use of the organization elements provided in an R/3 System. The available organization elements are fixed within the R/3 System. Therefore, configuration requires the selection of these elements of the enterprise structure in such a manner as to implement the organization arrangement of the specific company for which configuration is being performed. That is, it is necessary to map a company's organization structure to the available R/3 System–provided enterprise structure. Because this structure is used throughout the configuration process, it must be established early in configuration. Once established, it is not easily revised. The Project IMG facilitates the establishment of the organization arrangement during a company's configuration by defining that structure. (See **Figure 7.12.**)

FIGURE 7.12
R/3 System
Organization Units
IMG

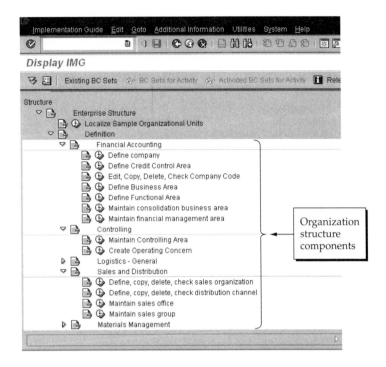

FIGURE 7.13
R/3 System
Organizational
Diagram

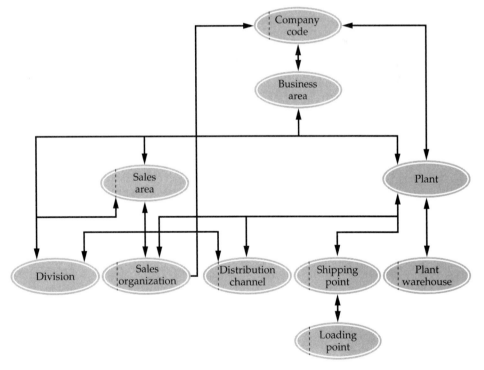

This R/3 System Enterprise Structure can be represented by an Organizational Diagram, which is a model of the relationships among the various R/3 System organizational elements (see **Figure 7.13**). It represents the organizational structure implemented within the R/3 System. This is the basis for the organizational arrangement of the chart of accounts and other reporting relationships within a company. During configuration a company maps its real-world organizational elements to the organizational elements available within the R/3 System. For example, if a company is organized as more than one legal entity, that relationship is included in the organizational structure and would be reflected in the Organizational Diagram. This organization structure is a required component of every configuration, regardless of the number of application modules that are implemented for a particular company. The reporting relationships of a global business are described by the Organizational Diagram. Whereas some R/3 System organizational elements, such as a company code, are required, others are optional and are specified when mapping a company's organizational structure to the available organizational elements of the SAP R/3 System.

To provide you with a general understanding of the enterprise structure, several of the key elements of the organizational diagram are described as follows:

- **Company code** is the identification number of an independent accounting unit that can generate its own financial statements. Legal entities are represented by company codes. As a legal requirement, a business that operates in several countries must establish a separate company code unit for each country.

- **Business area** is a subdivision of the company code that further subdivides the account transactions posted to the general ledger of the parent company code, but has to be reconciled with it. The business area is not an independent business unit, although it will manage the transaction data and the financial results shown in the company code balance sheet and the profit and loss statement, insofar as they concern its own business area.

- **Plant** is an organizational element that is used to provide standardized, independent, detailed production planning for areas of a company that have a high degree of integration from a production perspective. Plants are assigned to each distribution channel/sales organization combination. A plant is uniquely assigned to one company code. Within a plant, a **plant warehouse** is an organizational unit used to maintain materials that are stored in different locations.

- **Sales organization** is a subarea for assigning all the revenues of a sales organization. The revenues of a sales organization are assigned to only one company code.

- **Sales area** is a subdivision of a sales organization that is used to specify the responsibility for the sale and distribution of materials that are assigned to a certain **division** and can be distributed via a certain **distribution channel.** Sales areas are formed by combining a sales organization, a distribution channel, and a division.

- **Shipping point** is an organizational unit at a fixed location that carries out shipping activities. For example, a shipping point could be a company's mail department or a plant's rail depot. Each delivery is processed by only one shipping point. The **loading point** is the physical location within a shipping point where goods are loaded for shipment.

The available organizational elements are the same regardless of whether the R/3 System is being implemented for a manufacturing company or for an organization that is a service industry, such as a utility company or a college or university. For a nonmanufacturing organization, considerable creativity is often applied in mapping the company's organizational structure to the available R/3 System organizational elements. This mapping is a significant undertaking that needs to be performed early in the configuration process so the organizational structure has been defined and is available for use with other configuration activities.

ABAP Development Workbench

The ABAP Development Workbench is an integrated set of fourth-generation tools that support the implementation of critical client/server applications, enhancement of delivered applications, or add-ons to standard R/3 System modules. Customer-developed processes take place here, such as those illustrated previously in **Figure 7.3**. Recall, **ABAP** stands for Advanced Business Application Programming. The major components of the ABAP Development Workbench include ABAP Programming Language, ABAP Dictionary, ABAP Editor, ABAP Function Library, Data Modeler, R/3 Repository, Screen Painter, and Menu Painter. The ABAP Development Workbench is SAP's integrated tool set for the development of enterprisewide client/server applications. This tool set is especially suited to R/3 System installations that require enhancements to standard R/3 business applications with customized add-on functionality. This Development Workbench with its set of component tools is part of the SAP Web AS included in the NetWeaver platform, as portrayed previously in **Figure 7.4**. Key features provided by the ABAP Development Workbench include standardized access to databases, communications to external applications, international capabilities, and online documentation to support this tool set. If the standard business processes of the R/3 System do not include the required functionality for a particular company, it can be created using the ABAP Development Workbench. All of the business processes of the R/3 System application modules are created using the ABAP programming language. Extensions to these capabilities, such as those for industry solutions, are also written in the ABAP programming language using this Development Workbench.

The ABAP programming language is distinctive among enterprise software systems for the following reasons:

- The ABAP language, with the SAP R/3 Repository and the other individual development tools, provides an integrated architecture for the development of new programs and the creation of enhancements to the existing SAP R/3 Enterprise components.
- The developer does not need to be familiar with the technical details of the overall system environment, such as the operating system, database management system, network, or client/server communications.
- Structured programming is supported, with all the elements for modularizing programs and for creating business objects.
- The ABAP language is portable across operating systems and database management systems because the programs are translated into optimal internal representation, which is interpreted at runtime.
- The data is controlled by the ABAP Data Dictionary, which can be altered independently of the programs because they are regenerated automatically under control of the dictionary.
- The scope of the language is tailored to the context of business information systems and processing of business transactions.
- The ABAP programming language is designed with multilingual capabilities to meet the demands of worldwide system development, including requirements to ensure that different end-user language requirements are readily integrated in the programs for the common business processes. This capability is implemented by using language-dependent text elements.

FIGURE 7.14
Sample ABAP
Program

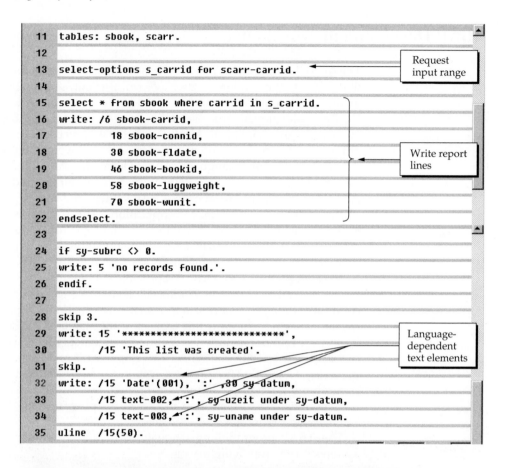

```
11    tables: sbook, scarr.
12
13    select-options s_carrid for scarr-carrid.        ◄──── Request
14                                                            input range
15    select * from sbook where carrid in s_carrid.
16    write: /6 sbook-carrid,
17            18 sbook-connid,
18            30 sbook-fldate,                          ◄──── Write report
19            46 sbook-bookid,                                lines
20            58 sbook-luggweight,
21            70 sbook-wunit.
22    endselect.
23
24    if sy-subrc <> 0.
25    write: 5 'no records found.'.
26    endif.
27
28    skip 3.
29    write: 15 '****************************',        Language-
30            /15 'This list was created'.             dependent
31    skip.                                            text elements
32    write: /15 'Date'(001), ':', /30 sy-datum,
33            /15 text-002, ':', sy-uzeit under sy-datum,
34            /15 text-003, ':', sy-uname under sy-datum.
35    uline  /15(50).
```

FIGURE 7.15
Selection Entry
Screen for Sample
ABAP Program

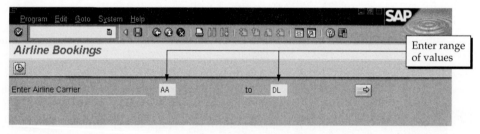

A sample ABAP program is shown in **Figure 7.14.** This program presents a value range selection screen to the end user (see **Figure 7.15**). The user makes the selection, and the list report displays for the user (see **Figure 7.16**). The SELECT statement shown in **Figure 7.14** is a structured query language (SQL) command that obtains the specified data from the SAP R/3 database.

In **Figure 7.14,** text elements are used to obtain language-dependent text in lines 32, 33, and 34 of the program. Line 32 includes a default text element value of "Date" that is used in the event one is not specified for a particular end-user language. The text elements appear in the list report based on the user's logon language.

To sum up, the SAP R/3 System includes a number of built-in tools, such as the Reference Model, the IMG, and ABAP. These tools support the various activities conducted to configure and install an SAP R/3 Enterprise System in an organization.

FIGURE 7.16
List Report from
Sample ABAP
Program

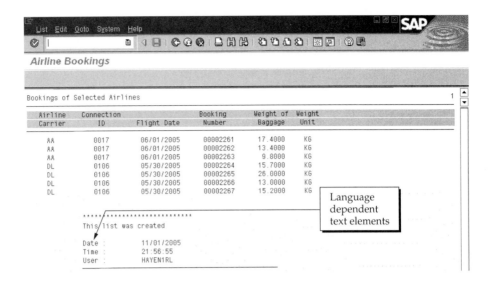

Quick Check

1. True or false: Configuration is the process of selecting and matching the available SAP business processes with a competitor's order management requirements.

2. List three primary configuration support tools for SAP R/3 Enterprise.

3. True or false: Customizing is a fine-tuning activity carried out on an R/3 installation that is already running a prototype form.

4. The _____ is used to identify, document, and represent existing enterprise-specific business processes in the R/3 System.

5. List three different components stored in the R/3 Repository.

6. True or false: The IMG provides detailed menus for configuring and setting R/3 application modules.

7. The _____ is an integrated set of fourth-generation tools that support the development of add-ons to the standard R/3 System.

8. True or false: The R/3 System has a totally flexible enterprise structure that can be varied in a unique arrangement for each company's configuration.

9. List the three instances of a three-system landscape architecture.

10. A _____ application makes extensive use of relatively static data that is stored in a file or database for using in controlling processing of this type of application software.

Chapter 8

Implementation Framework

Project Team Structure

The implementation of an SAP R/3 Enterprise System in a company is similar to many other information system development activities. It follows the **systems development life cycle** (SDLC), which is a generally accepted procedure for creating information systems that are widely deployed in organizations.

The **Accelerated SAP** (ASAP) methodology is a specialized arrangement of the SDLC that is adapted to the particular activities involved with an R/3 System implementation delivered using SAP Solution Manager. A project team assumes the responsibilities and functions of carrying out the various activities needed to implement an R/3 System. Recall, this is a significant information system undertaking, because many existing computer-based systems capabilities are being replaced and/or improved. The team responsible for this requires support from three major sources: (1) committed management, (2) users with knowledge of business functions and requirements, and (3) consultants with knowledge of the R/3 System and the management of its installation.

This team must be empowered to make the decisions required when business requirements are mapped into R/3 business processes and their functionality. Consultants provide specialized project methodology, project tracking, and techniques for executing the project, and they understand the methodology and tools that are inherent to SAP. Consultants bring their experience with the R/3 System and its configuration, including the system architecture, functionality, integration, and programming language that are unique to SAP. They can shorten the users' learning curve and provide knowledge transfer that reduces project risk and that accelerates project delivery.

The project team has responsibilities that include:

- Assessing how the R/3 Enterprise System and companion SAP products, if needed, will enable the business processes
- Identifying the impact on, and requirements for, business processes to support the enterprise "To-Be" vision with the R/3 System
- Designing the integration of the R/3 System organizational structure and configuration across the company
- Ensuring an efficient transfer of knowledge throughout the project

FIGURE 8.1
Project Team Structure

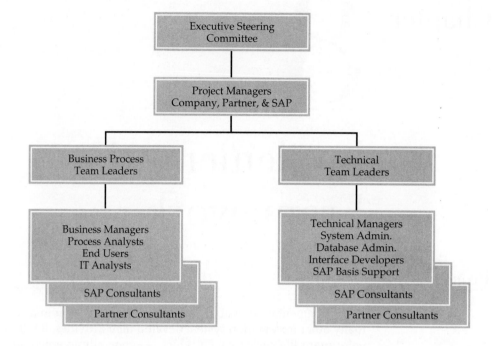

The project team structure (see **Figure 8.1**) is comprised of managers, analysts, and end users who are supported by consultants to enable effective knowledge transfer. The roles and responsibilities of the team are described next.

Executive steering committee. They are responsible for setting priorities, approving the project scope, and deciding enterprisewide issues. This committee commits the resources to the project. They monitor the progress of the project and assess the organizational impacts from the project. This team function empowers the other members of the team to make decisions regarding the details of the configuration and implementation.

Project managers. The project managers are charged with the overall management of the project and define the project parameters relative to the company and its information technology (IT) strategies. This responsibility includes the details of project organization and planning, and is carried out in collaboration with SAP AG and/or partner consultants. This team function determines the other staffing assignments for the project team from both company and consulting perspectives. That is, when SAP AG consultants are used, a manager from SAP AG is assigned the responsibility of the project for those consultants and their interactions with the company's team members.

Team leaders. They work with the project manager to plan and manage the project scope, resources, and schedule. Their work includes identifying the impact on requirements for integrated business processes to support the company's To-Be vision with the R/3 System. They identify the impact on and requirements for jobs and teams. Team leader responsibilities are divided between the business processes and the technical infrastructure. The **business process team leaders** are tasked with the implementation of the appropriate R/3 System business processes to meet business requirements. The **technical team leaders** are responsible for the installation of the hardware that will run the R/3 System and of the actual R/3 System software to provide the technical delivery platform of the R/3 System.

Process analysts. They work with the **business managers** and **end users** of the business processes to design the specific solution for the company based on the business requirements and R/3 System functionality for the To-Be processing vision. They map the company's requirements to the available processes in the R/3 System as defined by the Reference Structure. Then they perform the actual configuration of the R/3 System using the IMG to implement those processes. Test cases for validating the selected business processes are created and run to ensure the desired business requirements are met. Requirements for end-user training and support are determined and developed.

IT analysts. They configure the R/3 System to meet business processing requirements with a focus on designing interfaces for the end users. They design and develop the conversion approach for moving from the old system to the new system implemented with the R/3 System. Their concern is with the technical aspects of the business processes determined by the process analysts to ensure the business processes will provide the required functionality.

System administrators. They define the computer hardware and network requirements that provide the technology platform on which the R/3 System will run. Their responsibilities include the actual installation of the SAP R/3 System application software. They administer and maintain the R/3 System data including creating user names and passwords and performing backups of the data. Their work includes the **SAP R/3 Basis** or NetWeaver support for installing any system updates, such as **hot patches,** that are fixes for known difficulties or for improvements in the R/3 System.

Database administrators. They are responsible for the data model and any changes to the SAP R/3 database. Some of the requirements determined by the process analysts and the IT analysts may require the addition of new fields to the existing R/3 database. This function is responsible for managing, coordinating, and implementing those changes.

Interface developers. This technical staff creates ABAP report and dialog programs that provide enhanced interfaces for end users or to other non-SAP applications. These enhancements satisfy the requirements specified by the IT analysts working with the process analysts to meet the processing needs of the company.

As the implementation project progresses, the knowledge transfer from the consultants to the company's team members should increase, so that the need for the consultants is decreased as the capabilities of the company's team members increase. Eventually, the need for the consultants on the project should be phased out, with the company's team members assuming full responsibility for the ongoing maintenance of the R/3 System.

System Development Life Cycle

The SDLC is a generally accepted methodology, or organized process, that can be followed in developing and implementing computer-based information systems in an organization. The SDLC is frequently adapted to different kinds of information systems implementations in organizations. Accelerated SAP is an SDLC methodology that has been created to guide the rapid implementation of the R/3

Enterprise System. The steps of the ASAP methodology detail the specific events and activities that must be performed to successfully complete an SAP configuration. Although ASAP has unique names for its steps, these have many similarities to those of the SDLC. Project team members should have an understanding of these similarities so that they can draw upon this prior knowledge of information systems projects in carrying out an SAP R/3 implementation using ASAP or another project methodology provided by a consulting company.

The primary objectives of an SDLC and of the ASAP methodology are to:

- Define tasks to be carried out in an information systems project.
- Introduce consistency among information system development projects within an organization and facilitate communication.
- Provide common checkpoints for control of the project.

The SDLC for custom-built software provides the foundation for comparison to other development methodologies including ASAP. The SDLC (see **Figure 8.2**) is delineated as a series of seven steps. Although the SDLC may be defined with more or fewer steps, the seven steps represent the essence of most information system development projects. Each of the steps or phases is described next.

Problem recognition. End users identify a business need or opportunity, which may be addressed with a new or improved computer-based information system. Resources are requested and a management commitment obtained for developing a new system, such as that obtained from an executive steering committee for an R/3 System implementation.

Define user requirements. The users' overall information needs for responding to identified business needs or opportunities are determined. This establishes what the system is supposed to do. These activities are similar to those that are the responsibility of the process analysts for an R/3 System implementation.

Analyze existing system. The current system or business operations are examined to determine the detailed requirements for the new system. The

FIGURE 8.2
System Development Life Cycle

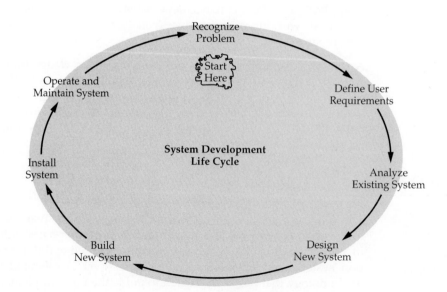

technological, economic, operational, and organizational feasibility of the system is evaluated. Alternative approaches are formulated and evaluated to select the most appropriate option.

Design new system. A specification or blueprint of the new system is prepared that details the specific input, output, processing, and storage requirements of the system.

Build new system. The system is coded and tested. A 3GL, 4GL, DBMS, or some combination of these may be used in coding the new system.

Install system. Final testing is completed, end users are trained, data is converted from any existing system, cut-over occurs, and use of the new system begins.

Operate and maintain system. The system is used to meet the information processing needs of the company. End users enter data and receive reports or other related outputs. Adjustments are made to the system to keep it current with changing business requirements, such as a change in legal reporting requirements.

A general knowledge of this SDLC is valuable when information requirements and project progress are conveyed to professional system analysts, to programmers, or to configuration specialists, regardless of whether the business system is R/3 Enterprise or some other system. When an SAP R/3 System is being implemented in a company, the ability to articulate the steps of the ASAP methodology in the more familiar terminology of the SDLC of the company enhances communication. Furthermore, not every employee is likely to be an SAP R/3 project team member. Therefore, the project team members should be able to relate their project activities to activities that are familiar to others in the company.

The SDLC can be adjusted to the activities of an R/3 System or to other enterprise software implementation (see **Figure 8.3**). The process of selecting and installing the R/3 Enterprise software is not included in this SDLC, which concentrates on the configuration activities. The decision to use the R/3 System and the

FIGURE 8.3
SDLC with Enterprise Software

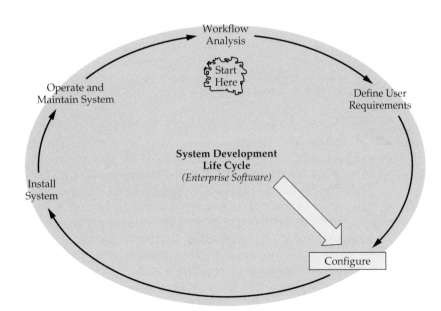

installation of the technology platform—that is, the hardware and software—would usually precede this arrangement of the SDLC.

For this SDLC with enterprise software, the Recognize Problem phase is replaced with a Workflow Analysis step. The traditional SDLC phases of Analyze Existing System, Design New System, and Build New System are replaced by the Configure step, as indicated in **Figure 8.3.** However, many of the project tasks in the SDLC with enterprise software remain similar to those of the traditional SDLC. It is these similarities that can be leveraged in the communication processes among SAP project team members and other company employees during an R/3 System implementation.

Prototyping

Prototyping is a system development methodology in which end users are provided with a working model of what a proposed information system will be like before it is built. This allows end users to test-drive a version of the system and lets them assess whether the system meets their requirements. The prototype usually goes through several cycles of revisions as it is refined to better meet end-user requirements. Each cycle consists of these activities:

- Analysis of requirements
- Design of input, output, and processing specifications
- Building or programming of the specification to produce an operating version of the system

At the end of each cycle, the resulting system is demonstrated to the end users and their approval is requested. At the end of the first several cycles, the users are expected to provide direction for improving the system. The revisions are made in the next cycle of the prototyping process. When the system satisfies the user requirements, prototyping is finished, and provisions are made for moving the system into production. This general prototyping cycle can be modified for an approach that provides a common method of configuring an R/3 System (see **Figure 8.4**). Accelerated SAP uses cycles to add functionality for an initial, baseline configuration. For an SAP Configuration, prototyping occurs throughout these cycles, in which BPPs are added to the configuration at each cycle.

The prototyping cycle for an SAP installation involves reviewing the workflow or business processing requirements so they can be configured and then tested. Each cycle is designed around a grouping of R/3 business processes that can be configured and tested together. This requires planning in the selection of the processes configured in any one cycle. With each cycle more processes are included until the final requirements are satisfied. The added processes permit testing and experimentation by the users to identify areas that may require additional attention. This follows the iterative approach of the traditional prototyping cycle, but represents the adjustment of that method to the configuration of enterprise software. Knowledge about the application of prototyping to other information systems can be used to help communicate the cycles of configuration activities for the SAP R/3 implementation.

These configuration activities can provide an R/3 System installation approach that follows either the big bang approach or a phased implementation. The **big bang approach** occurs when one or more SAP application modules are implemented throughout an entire enterprise, such as all accounting modules or all logistics

FIGURE 8.4
Prototyping Cycle
for Enterprise
Software

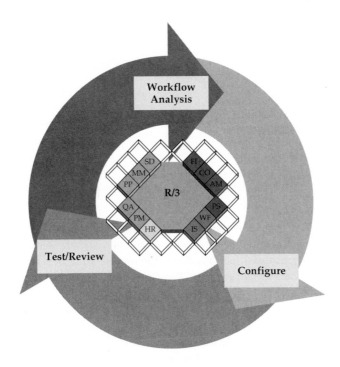

modules available in the R/3 System. The **phased implementation approach** occurs when SAP components are implemented step by step, over time. This phasing may take place by application module, by site and physical location, by business unit, or by material or customer type.

Solution Manager Implementation

Solution Manager is the SAP platform that delivers the ASAP methodology. ASAP is an SAP R/3 implementation methodology that is an SDLC tailored specifically to R/3 System installations. This method seeks to standardize and expedite the typical R/3 System implementation. It is tightly linked to the R/3 System business processing functions, with tools or accelerators provided that collect the information necessary to configure the R/3 System business processes. This standard SDLC makes it easier to use consultants more effectively among different projects and to provide an increased level of consistency. It results in a repeatable SDLC "model" that can be used across different implementations of the R/3 System.

Solution Manager includes accelerators for carrying out many of the tasks required to implement an R/3 System using the ASAP methodology. The project implementation tools provided by Solution Manager could be created from scratch or from a company's standard SDLC for use with a company's R/3 System installation. However, the time and effort required to develop the tools used for these activities are usually better invested directly in the configuration process, rather than in the development of tools that use a different or company-specific information systems development methodology. The accelerators are provided at a low level that walks the project team members through hands-on tasks of the configuration.

FIGURE 8.5
Accelerated SAP
Roadmap

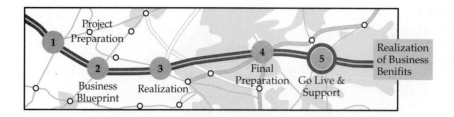

The ASAP methodology delivered by Solution Manager is described by its Roadmap, which divides the implementation process into five phases or steps (see **Figure 8.5**). Each of these Roadmap phases is described next.

Phase 1: Project Preparation. The primary focus of this phase is getting the project started, identifying team members, and developing a high-level plan. In an executive kickoff meeting, the project team and business process managers obtain a clear sense of their roles and responsibilities throughout the project. This phase also includes technical requirement planning that determines the necessary hardware for the R/3 System implementation.

Phase 2: Business Blueprint. The focus of this phase is requirements gathering. The key deliverable for the phase is a requirements document or Business Blueprint that is approved by middle management. The purpose of this phase is to define and understand the business goals of the company and to determine the business processes required to support those goals. The Business Blueprint is used to finalize the detailed scope of the project. These activities are similar to those of the "define user requirements" step of the traditional SDLC; however, they are tailored specifically to an R/3 System installation. ASAP accelerators are used to gather the requirements for the Business Blueprint. This includes the detailed requirements for IMG processes and master data, such as those for the customer master, the material master, number ranges, units of measure, and payment terms.

Phase 3: Realization. The main activities of this phase involve the implementation of the business processing requirements based on the Business Blueprint. A first working version of the configuration is prepared. This is similar to a first working model with prototyping. The organizational structure is specified in this phase. A preconfigured client may be used in creating a baseline R/3 System that represents the business processes identified in the Business Blueprint phase. A **preconfigured client** is a template configuration that contains common or industry-specific configuration settings in order to jump-start the customizing activities. With a preconfigured client, standard R/3 System business transactions can be run as soon as the client is installed. This makes it useful as a demonstration tool during requirements analysis in creating the Business Blueprint. This playback of the business processes to the project team allows for feedback and further confirmation that the requirements defined in the Business Blueprint are being satisfied. It represents the completion of the first cycle of the ASAP prototyping approach.

Following an initial baseline system configuration, it is evolved into an integrated and documented solution that fulfills all the processing requirements of the Business Blueprint. Throughout this phase, the configuration of each core business process is divided into iterations or cycles of related business process flows. The business process flows are configured in parallel with the development of reports, user procedures, testing scenarios, and security profiles. Cycles are small, coordinated groups of configuration, testing, and training for the business process procedures (BPPs).

Groups of BPPs that are recommended for the same cycle are indicated in the BPP Master List, which is an ASAP accelerator. These cycles provide milestones for the project team and establish checkpoints to test a playback of specific parts of the overall business process. This approach provides immediate feedback and involves the entire company throughout the project. The cycles provide a prototyping approach that continually builds and refines each business process and its configuration until the To-Be business solution has been realized.

A **configuration freeze**—that is, halting the configuration processes—occurs at the end of the realization phase in order to prepare the production environment for final tests. This provides the final configuration of the company's R/3 System for the start of production. Additional configuration is still possible. However, any configuration after this freeze would be carried out using the development client and then using the transport facility of the R/3 System to provide for the QA testing before moving any changes into production. The primary deliverable from this phase is a successfully configured R/3 System that is ready for testing and validation.

Phase 4: Final Preparation. The primary activities of this phase are to complete final system testing, train end users, and to cut over both the data and the system to a production environment. Final system testing consists of testing conversion procedures and programs, testing interface programs, conducting volume and stress tests, and conducting final user acceptance tests. The final activity of this phase is to gain approval of the system and the readiness of the company to go live—that is, to officially turn on the SAP R/3 Enterprise System that has been configured to the requirements of the company based on the Business Blueprint.

Phase 5: Go Live and Support. This phase consists of the ongoing support for the R/3 System. Immediately after the go-live event, the production system should be reviewed and refined to ensure that the business environment is fully supported. Business results and system performance should be measured and reviewed so any difficulties can be addressed and corrective actions taken. The system can continue to be rolled out to additional levels, and the use of additional features can be achieved in a controlled manner. A new release of the R/3 System can trigger actions that require an upgrade to the R/3 System modules. In that case, much of the same planning and implementation that occurred for the initial implementation is repeated for the upgrade. However, since an upgrade is usually a refinement of the existing configuration, the total effort is significantly less than that for the initial configuration and can usually be accomplished with little or no need for consultants.

Overall, ASAP is an SDLC methodology that is specifically tailored to the implementation of the R/3 System using cycles of a prototyping approach. Solution Manager furnishes ASAP accelerators, which provide a step-by-step guide that supports a repeatable implementation process and reduces the risks inherent in an R/3 System implementation.

Quick Check

1. True or false: Enterprise software is packaged software that is configured to the requirements of a particular company without the need to modify the programs provided by the software vendor.

2. _____ is an SAP R/3 implementation methodology that seeks to standardize and expedite a typical R/3 configuration.

3. List the five phases of the Accelerated SAP Roadmap.

4. Baseline and final configuration occurs in the _____ phase of the Roadmap.

5. The Conduct System Test is a work package that is included in the _____ phase of the Roadmap.

6. After go live, _____ occurs to provide the upgrades needed to meet ongoing business requirements.

7. True or false: A preconfigured client is only useful for end-user training and usually increases the duration of the R/3 configuration activities.

8. The _____ phase of the Accelerated SAP Roadmap usually requires the greatest amount of effort.

Chapter 9

Organization Structure

Enterprise Data Model

The **Enterprise Data Model** is a schema or map of the overall logical structure of a database. A **database** is a store of integrated data capable of being directly accessed for multiple uses. It is organized so that various business transactions can be accessed through a single reference, based on relationships among the records in the database tables. The SAP R/3 Enterprise System is implemented using relational database technology that utilizes table-driven processing. In the R/3 System this is a global representation that controls the organizational arrangement and use of the R/3 System data. This logical representation provides a complete description of the business entities and relationships for a database.

During configuration a company's organization structure must be analyzed and mapped to the predefined, available structure provided within the R/3 database. This organization structure provides the primary implementation framework for all the transaction data of the R/3 System. In learning about the SAP R/3 Enterprise System, you need to learn about the predefined database structure provided with the R/3 System to classify transactions for appropriate business units and their reporting requirements. This understanding is especially necessary to configure the R/3 System and for its ongoing maintenance, because a company might reorganize its business units and change reporting relationships within the company.

The R/3 System uses logical databases that have predefined paths for accessing database tables. To effectively access data in the R/3 System database, the data must be arranged around the organizational structure of the various business units that make up a particular company. The organizational elements of the R/3 System provide this arrangement of the data for use with the R/3 application modules. Once a company's requirements are mapped to these predefined paths, the database tables are available for use by the various transaction and report programs across the R/3 application modules. Different application modules access a database view of the relevant tables for that application. A **view** represents a relational database method for generating application-oriented cross-sections of data stored in the database tables.

Logical database design is a way of identifying and quantifying the key features of a database. This design examines the business requirements and transforms those requirements into a database design. Although the R/3 System is installed with a predefined database structure, the exact use of many of the key fields in the database must be determined for a specific implementation of an R/3 System.

FIGURE 9.1 General Ledger Account Data Model

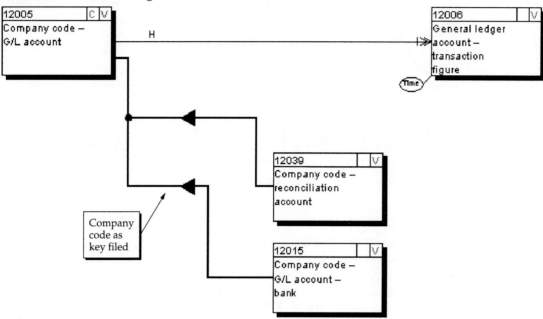

A **data model** is a logical representation of the data structure of a database that is used to specify business entities and their relationship in a meaningful way. A data model provides the framework or mental image of how a company's data requirements are related and is generally expressed using a diagram. Thus, a data model diagram is a graphical representation of entities and their relationship for a database. **Figure 9.1** is an example graphical diagram of the data model for the General Ledger Account (BUS3006).

A **bubble diagram** is one method used to display a graphical representation of entities and their relationships. This method provides a data model that is useful in communicating representations of data structures among project participants. The diagram of the R/3 organizational view (refer to **Figure 7.4** in Chapter 7) is a bubble diagram.

Configuration includes setting up the R/3 System database to support a company's transaction processing and management reporting requirements. This provides a framework for the data used in the R/3 implementation and determines the table-driven application data, which is relatively permanent data used by the R/3 System for a particular organization. To configure an R/3 System, the development team must understand:

- The database tables available in the R/3 System
- The business requirements of the organizational structure in which transactions are processed and management reports are produced
- How to use the R/3 System configuration tools that are available for setting up the database tables that describe the company's reporting

For someone new to the R/3 System to effectively participate in an SAP installation, he or she needs to learn about the SAP database tables and elements that must be specified to configure much of the master data for the R/3 System.

Customer order management (COM) is a common process in most companies. COM begins when a customer places an order and ends when payment is received. COM transactions must share data that is organized to meet business reporting requirements. This processing is supported by the R/3 System by use of data and business functions that record and handle the information required to complete the processing. This data is stored in one or more relational database tables in the R/3 database, where a **table** is a collection of database records of the same type. In the relational database model that is used with the R/3 System, these tables are a two-dimensional arrangement of rows and columns in which rows represent records and the columns represent fields. For COM, a database record is used to store the information for each customer transaction. Similar data storage occurs for the other transactions of the R/3 application modules. For COM, business transaction processing requires the integration of data throughout the various business functions and their application modules needed to complete this processing. These organizational elements, which are represented by the Enterprise Data Model (see **Figure 9.2**), provide a framework for the database that is used to describe these transactions with respect to key data fields that uniquely identify the transaction. These identifying elements include product or part number, customer number, business area, sales area, and plant.

A key factor in the configuration and implementation of the R/3 System is determining the organizational elements for the R/3 System. The specification of these elements is used in configuring master data in the R/3 System database.

FIGURE 9.2   Conceptual Enterprise Data Model

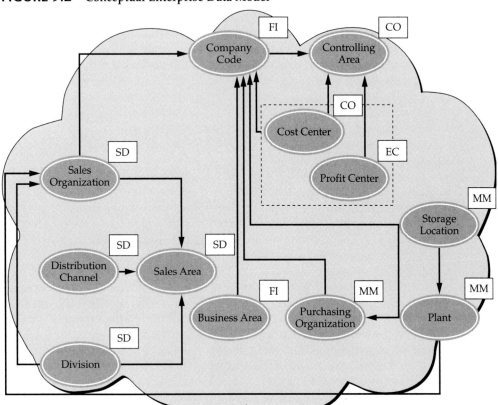

Once the data is entered in the database, significant effort may be required to rearrange the data for a different organizational structure. It is important to thoroughly analyze the organizational structure and its related reporting requirements before entering this master data in the R/3 System. Mapping a company's organization structure to that provided in the R/3 System often requires creative thinking concerning the organizational entity requirements. This is where the experience of consultants can be very useful to a new R/3 System configuration.

Enterprise Structure and Organizational Elements

The SAP Reference IMG is a view of the Enterprise Structure that describes the relationship among the predefined organizational elements of the R/3 System database. This is the framework on which all data is organized in the R/3 System database. During implementation a company maps its organizational elements to the SAP Enterprise Structure designed into the R/3 System. In the R/3 System, organizational elements form structures that represent the legal and organizational views of a company.

A **logical user view,** also known as a **user view,** is a representation of the R/3 System data that users need to process transactions, to answer inquiries, or to make decisions. Each of the R/3 application modules has its unique logical user view of the data in the R/3 System database. These logical user views are provided through the implementation framework of the organizational structure. The data in the R/3 System database is related to specific business transactions and is grouped by the organizational elements that specify the structure of the business units. The organizational structure is realized by a company's use of the key fields in the database tables. These organizational elements establish the database foundation on which transactions of the R/3 System are implemented. In preparation for establishing the company's organization structure, it is useful to understand the primary logical user views within a client of the R/3 System, which are as follows:

- Financial accounting
- Controlling (manufacturing planning and execution)
- Sales and distribution
- Materials management

Organizational views are presented through the Enterprise Structure in the IMG. The Enterprise Structure (see **Figure 9.3**) displays the entities that are specified within a selected application module. Recall that the key fields in the R/3 System database are predefined. A company does not create its own fields; rather, it determines their use and provides the actual values that describe the company's organizational structure.

When an R/3 System configuration is complete, a series of tables contains the description of the company's organizational structure for its specific business units and their reporting relationships. These tables contain the relatively permanent data that drives or controls the processing of transactions. Mapping a company's organization structure to the predefined R/3 System database organization structure is a key activity in fitting the company's reporting requirements into the R/3 System. If a company is considering revising its organization structure as part of an R/3 System implementation, this needs to be accomplished early in the configuration of the R/3 System. In mapping a company's organization structure to the predefined R/3

FIGURE 9.3
Enterprise Structure
Delineates
Organization
Elements

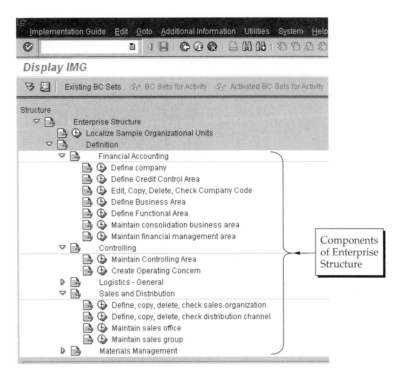

System organization structure, these factors need to be considered:

- The intended use of the R/3 System organizational elements
- The business processing and information requirements of the company
- The relationship or mapping between the R/3 System's intended use and a company's use

Some organizational elements are considered as **core organizational elements** because they are used in all business processes and application modules. The core organizational elements are the client, the company code, the plant, and the business area.

The R/3 System is an integrated system based on accounting principles that support monitoring and controlling the value of a company. Information must be available in an arrangement that supports decision making about the best allocation of resources. The process of monitoring and controlling the value of a company is typically divided into financial (external) accounting and managerial (internal) accounting. Financial accounting occurs based on standard accounting principles and legal requirements. Managerial accounting is characterized by flexibility and by procedures that are not regulated by legal requirements. The company's organization structure must be established for meeting both the financial and managerial accounting requirements. That structure is then used to define the use of the predefined elements of the data structures in the R/3 System database.

The procedures for using the Enterprise Structure to configure the R/3 System are as follows:

- Understand the R/3 System database organizational elements as a guide in establishing the company's organization structure.
- Design the company's organization structure for use with the R/3 System to process transactions and produce managerial reports.

FIGURE 9.4
Financial
Accounting View

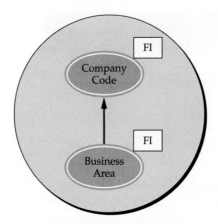

- Map the defined organization structure to the R/3 System database entities by matching a company's organization element with that available in the predefined R/3 System database.
- Enter the defined organization structure into the appropriate R/3 System database tables.

Financial Accounting View

This is the logical user view of the Financial Accounting (FI) application module. Primary organizational elements in this view are the company code and the business area (see **Figure 9.4**). The **company code** is a legal entity within an R/3 System client. Company codes define the structure that is used to prepare financial statements that include balance sheets and income statements. A key decision for the company code is determining the true legal entities of the company. The business area is used for flexible reporting across company codes. A **business area** is a special organizational element for which internal financial statements can be produced, such as a balance sheet and a profit and loss statement. A key decision for business areas is to determine whether to use the business area and how it will be defined for the company. The business area is an optional organizational element, whereas the company code is a required element. To illustrate this, consider the Motor Sports International (MSI) case example. MSI must produce a separate balance sheet and income statement for each of the U.S. and Canadian operations. Motorcycles and accessories are two distinct product lines that are manufactured at the operations in each country. What is an appropriate arrangement of the R/3 organizational elements for this business structure? A single R/3 client is used to represent the overall MSI company. The operations are legally independent entities located in these two geographical areas. A company code is assigned to each country. The product lines of motorcycles and accessories are mapped into the SAP business area element. For each product line the same business area is defined for the Canadian and U.S. operations. This allows MSI to produce combined business area reports for their North American operations as well as to prepare country-specific reports.

Controlling View

This is the logical user view of the Controlling (CO) application module that supports manufacturing planning and execution (see **Figure 9.5**). Different combinations of the components from the Controlling module can be configured to

FIGURE 9.5
Controlling View

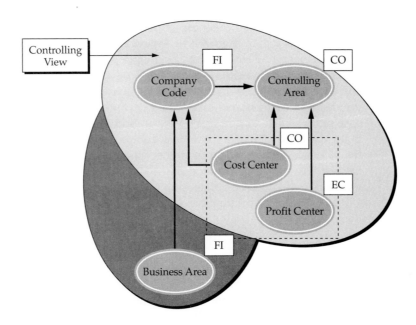

support the Enterprise Controlling (EC) module that facilitates comparing planned target performance with actual results for parts of the enterprise. Primary organizational elements in the Controlling view are the company code, the controlling area, the cost center, and the profit center. One company will see itself as a group of entirely independent business units reporting to a corporate office, whereas another company will think of the main functional areas, such as procurement, production, sales, and marketing. For the functional area arrangement, you need to define the organization in terms of a detailed structure of cost centers and profit centers, with specified relationships among them. This will provide reports that support the various controlling functions within the company. Although a company may have an existing controlling structure, that structure must be analyzed and then mapped to the predefined organizational structure in the R/3 database. A **controlling area** is an organizational unit within a company for which comprehensive, independent, management accounting can be performed. A controlling area can encompass several company codes operating in one or more currencies, where a group currency serves as the controlling area currency. When a controlling area contains more than one company code, then all company codes within that controlling area must use the same operational chart of accounts. A key decision for the controlling area is to define the internal management structure in order to identify and map that structure to the appropriate controlling areas of the R/3 database. The **cost center** represents a business entity to which costs are charged or allocated. This is the lowest level in the organization structure, where costs are collected and analyzed to evaluate the performance of the respective business unit. A **profit center** is a subdivision of a company code that is used for internal management control with enterprise controlling (EC). It is used to generate income statements and operating profit statements under various accounting methods.

Again consider the MSI situation. They manage and control their administrative budgets and costs across all companies (United States and Canada). The department is the lowest level within MSI for which costs and performances are monitored. They generate income statements and revenue and expense information for the paint and pumps product groups within the motorcycle product line. How should MSI map this business structure into the available SAP organizational structure? They map their North American management area to the SAP controlling area element. Departments are mapped to the SAP cost center elements. SAP profit centers are specified to support producing income statements for the paint and pumps product groups within the motorcycle product line. A list of values is prepared for each organizational element and entered in the appropriate R/3 database table. Notice that in this configuration activity the actual entry of the values in the database table is a trivial task compared with the effort required to arrive at the values to be entered in the table. This is typical of many configuration activities. That is, the determination of the values for the table-driven processing is the most difficult and time-consuming configuration activity, whereas entering those values in the appropriate table requires little effort.

Sales and Distribution View

This is the logical user view of the Sales and Distribution (SD) application module (see **Figure 9.6**). Primary organizational elements in this view are the company code, the sales organization, the distribution channel, the division, and the sales area. The **sales organization** is usually a geographic area or industry sector responsible for distributing goods or services and for negotiating sales. This area

FIGURE 9.6
Sales and Distribution View

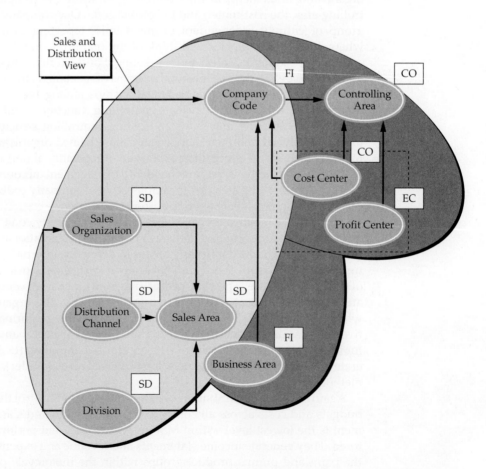

or sector is used in identifying each business transaction that is sales related and is entered for a sales order. A key decision for the sales organization is to determine whether one or multiple sales organizations are appropriate, where a single order cannot be processed for multiple sales organizations. The **distribution channel** is used to provide various means of supplying customers with their goods or services and is entered for each sales order. A key decision for the distribution channel is to determine if this level of flexibility is required beyond that provided by the sales organization. The **division** is used to group a sales material or product and is entered for each sales order. A key decision for divisions is to determine the impact of product line or sales material on the sales order–taking process to establish whether another level of flexibility is required for sales order processing. The **sales area** is an SAP organizational element that combines the sales organization, the distribution channel, and the division for a sales order to view sales-related master data. A key decision for the sales area is to determine if it is useful for reporting based on how it is derived from the other three organizational elements.

The elements of the Sales and Distribution view can be applied to MSI. They have a single sales organization with the U.S. operations and map this to the SAP sales organization element. A single channel of distribution is used, which is mapped to the SAP distribution channel element. The motorcycles and accessories product lines are mapped to the SAP division element to support reporting by these product lines. A list of the values for each of these organizational elements is prepared and entered in the appropriate R/3 database table. Again, the journey to determine the organizational structure elements and their values takes most of the effort, as compared with the nearly mechanical entry of those values in the R/3 System.

Materials Management View

This is the logical user view of the Materials Management (MM) application module (see **Figure 9.7**). Primary organizational elements in this view are the company code, the plant, the storage location, and the purchasing organization. The **plant** is an organizational element that is central to production planning and represents a location in which inventory quantities are stored or manufactured. This organizational unit is used in preparing material requirements planning (MRP) plans and in maintaining the associated inventories. A key decision for the plant is to determine the number of plants, which will be established in considering delivery processing and inventory analysis requirements. The **storage location** specifies a physical location within a plant where inventory is stored. A key decision for the storage location is to determine the number and identity of storage locations that will be used. The **purchasing organization** represents an organizational element that is responsible for the purchasing activities for one or more plants. This element is used to maintain vendor information that is used to generate purchase orders. A key decision for the purchasing organization is to determine whether one or multiple purchasing organizations will be established and how a company will create its purchase orders, such as in a centralized or decentralized way.

An example of a creative use of the predefined R/3 System Enterprise Structure is a commercial passenger airline. An airplane is an organization element that is central to production of airline passenger miles. As a result each aircraft is mapped to a plant (a predefined organizational element) in the R/3 System. An SAP AG or other experienced consultant is vital in understanding the use of a plant in the

FIGURE 9.7 Materials Management View

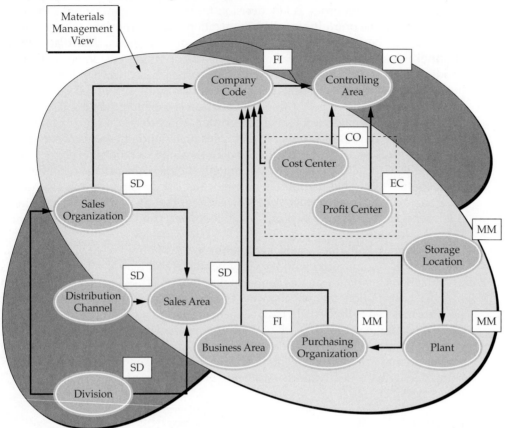

R/3 System, so that such a mapping can be made and results appropriately processed and reported.

Now consider the organization structure at MSI: They have two manufacturing plants within the U.S. operations. One plant produces and inventories motorcycles, while the other plant produces and inventories accessories. These two locations are mapped to the SAP plant organizational element. MSI has a single purchasing organization for its U.S. operations, which is mapped to the SAP purchasing organizational element and enables MSI to make purchases across all plants. Within a single manufacturing plant MSI has separate locations where inventories are stored. One area holds the raw materials, while the other area stores the finished goods. A storage location is specified for each of these physical locations. A list of the values for these organizational elements is prepared and entered into the R/3 database to specify the organizational structure for materials management at MSI.

The implementation framework for configuration is complete when the organizational elements for the Financial Accounting view, the Controlling view (manufacturing planning and execution), the Sales and Distribution view, and the Materials Management view have been established. This is performed early in the configuration activities so the organization structure is then available for the other configuration actions.

Quick Check

1. A key field is used to _____ identify the records in database tables.
2. The _____ is a map of the overall logical structure of a database.
3. True or false: A bubble diagram displays a graphical representation of the entities and their relationship in a database.
4. The _____ organizational element key field is used by *all* of the primary R/3 organizational views.
5. List the four primary organizational element views in SAP R/3.
6. The _____ organizational element is used to represent a location to which costs are charged or allocated.
7. The _____ organizational element is used to identify a geographical area or industry sector responsible for distributing goods or services and negotiating sales.
8. The _____ organizational element is used to identify a location in which inventory quantities and values are stored or manufactured.
9. The _____ organizational element is used to identify the various ways of supplying customers with their goods or services.
10. True or false: The predefined R/3 database field names should be renamed from their German names to match the organizational elements of a particular company.

Chapter 10

Customizing Tools

Solution Manager

SAP Solution Manager is useful in gathering information that is applied through the R/3 Reference Model to configure the R/3 Enterprise system. The R/3 Enterprise system and Solution Manager customization and configuration tools are used: (1) to gather the business requirements from the users and (2) to implement them in the R/3 System. These actions carry out an R/3 System configuration. The configured R/3 System, together with other SAP component products and non-SAP components, is run by an information technology function in an organization. These operations are facilitated by a holistic approach in which Solution Manager integrates various tools for development and ongoing maintenance. Solution Manager takes a consistent business process– and phase-oriented approach to manage a complete SAP solution through its entire life cycle. This is accomplished by furnishing a central knowledge depository within a business computing landscape. All information is pooled concerning the current solution in all phases of the life cycle. Information pooling eases communication between the information technology staff and the users/managers in the company's various lines of business. Solution Manager provides support throughout the complete life cycle of planning, implementation, operation, support, and continuous improvement for an R/3 Enterprise system.

Solution Manager provides seamless links to documents of the Accelerated SAP (ASAP) Roadmap, with point-and-click access, to facilitate their use by the project team members. The navigation pane in the main screen of Solution Manager provides direct access to any of the ASAP Roadmap phases by expanding these items. This navigation pane serves as a table of contents for Solution Manager activities. The user-procedure documents of Solution Manager also provide the base for user training and documentation. There are over 2,200 of these documents. Solution Manager provides access to several components that include:

- Implementation Roadmap
- Project plan
- Business process procedures

The Expanded Task Description view displays all the tasks included in the ASAP Roadmap. These are organized by the Roadmap phases, such as those for the Project Preparation (see **Figure 10.1**). The list presented can be expanded and is scrollable for all the other phases of the Roadmap and their related tasks. Selection of a link from the Expanded Task Description view displays the underlying detailed

FIGURE 10.1
Navigation within
Roadmaps

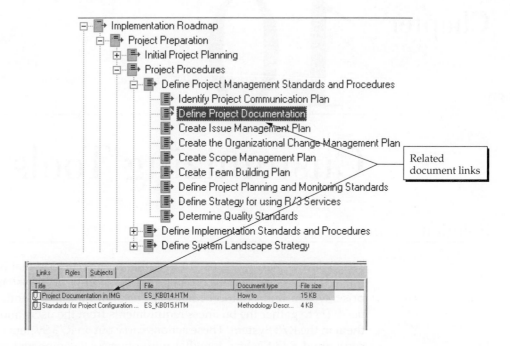

document. That document may in turn contain links to other specific Solution Manager documents that support the ASAP methodology. Ultimately, a document is reached that provides a detailed description of the particular configuration activity.

The Solution Manager Tool Kit includes the Implementation Roadmap with the various models, templates, questionnaires, and examples that are used to support the configuration process. This tool kit supports the configuration activities by using the Implementation Guide (IMG) and the Reference Model that are built into the R/3 System. That is, the Solution Manager Tool Kit collects the specific data needed to configure an R/3 System using the IMG and the Reference Model. This tool kit is a collection of **accelerators,** documents from various applications that include the Implementation Roadmap, Microsoft Word, Microsoft Excel, Microsoft PowerPoint, Adobe Acrobat, and HTML.

A document's format is selected to best implement the particular accelerator feature for the ASAP methodology of Solution Manager. A significant feature of the Word documents for the business process procedures (BPP) is that they are specifically keyed to the actual business processes in the R/3 System. The data collected with these accelerator documents is used to configure the corresponding business process. In some instances several BPP documents are necessary in order to collect all the information required to configure a single business process. HTML documents provide information similar to other tool kit documents; however, the HTML format reduces the amount of computer storage space required for the document and makes them readily accessible using a web browser. In the future, Solution Manager and its ASAP methodology will increase the use of HTML documents. PowerPoint templates are accelerators that allow the development team to more readily prepare for presentations regarding the implementation project, with a particular focus on supporting the project review meetings. These templates make it easier to prepare for the presentation. Portable Document Format (PDF) accelerators are more comprehensive documents that provide information on the configuration process, such as the "R/3 System Pre-Configured Client Made

Easy" document that contains over 100 pages and is a step-by-step guide to using an R/3 preconfigured client. Excel documents are template worksheets used as guides for the implementation team—for instance, the Project Scope Worksheet, which is used for recording the extent of the current R/3 System configuration. For example, the Project Scope Worksheet is used to record the plan of the business processes selected for the initial configuration. Once that is complete, additional processes may be added to that configuration. All the business process modules are included in the template, so the team needs to mark only those that will be used with the particular configuration. These accelerators in the ASAP Tool Kit expedite the configuration process, and their comprehensiveness ensures that all business processes are considered and evaluated for the configuration. This reduces the risk of overlooking a business process during the configuration activities.

Solution Manager Evolution

The SAP Solution Manager has evolved from Accelerated SAP. ASAP provides SAP customers and consultants with a standard methodology for implementing an R/3 System. In many instances ASAP replaced a unique implementation method developed and used by a specific consulting company. This presented a problem in providing consulting assistance to a wide variety of business customers. A technical support person who moved from the installation of one R/3 System to another was faced with two problems: (1) the technical issues and (2) understanding the development methodology being followed. There was no standard development roadmap. Without such a standard "playbook," it is difficult to know the current status of the implementation process. The technician had to understand the particular development methodology to provide appropriate technical assistance. With the advent of ASAP, configuration support personnel could now focus immediately and more effectively on the technical issues of the implementation. So, ASAP was a significant step forward in providing a repeatable and standardized R/3 System implementation process.

ASAP standardized the R/3 System implementation process by establishing a common implementation methodology and by providing accelerators. These accelerators are a generally accepted means for collecting the data needed for an R/3 System configuration. An implementation team then just selects the appropriate accelerator and uses it, rather than creating their own unique way of documenting requirements for the implementation. The information and data collected using ASAP was then used to manually make the configuration settings in the R/3 System. As an offline personal computer–based system, it had no direct connection to the R/3 System. A human intermediary was required. This led to the continued development of the ASAP methodology and tool kit (see **Figure 10.2**). The second iteration of the ASAP methodology resulted in ValueSAP. ValueSAP includes an enhanced and refined tool kit. Also, a direct connection was provided from the Business Process Procedure Master List to the R/3 System being configured. This permitted the selection of business process procedures in ValueSAP and the enabling of those selected processes in the R/3 System without the need for a person to make those selection entries in the IMG. The third major iteration of the ASAP methodology is SAP Solution Manager. This runs using the SAP Web AS platform, which is the same platform that runs the R/3 Enterprise system. The result is a much tighter integration between the ASAP methodology and the R/3 System configuration settings in the IMG. Solution Manager is the preferred

FIGURE 10.2
From ASAP to SAP
Solution Manager

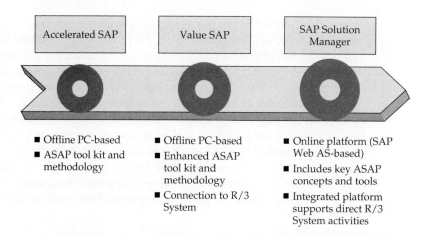

- ■ Offline PC-based
- ■ ASAP tool kit and methodology

- ■ Offline PC-based
- ■ Enhanced ASAP tool kit and methodology
- ■ Connection to R/3 System

- ■ Online platform (SAP Web AS-based)
- ■ Includes key ASAP concepts and tools
- ■ Integrated platform supports direct R/3 System activities

FIGURE 10.3
BPP Master List

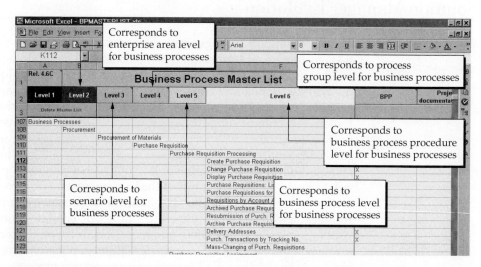

means of configuration setting. It facilitates making those choices within its ASAP methodology tool kit and having those choices transferred more seamlessly to the IMG than the earlier ASAP efforts did. The net result of this is that the selection of appropriate business processes leads directly to completed IMG settings, while greatly minimizing the need for human intervention beyond the selection of the business processes necessary to fulfill business requirements. The future direction of the entire SAP product suite is to continue to build on the use of Solution Manager in the implementation process that configures an R/3 Enterprise system or other SAP products.

BPP Master List

The Business Process Procedure (BPP) Master List is an Excel workbook ASAP tool that contains a listing of the business processes that are available in the R/3 System for a planned configuration. Business processes are selected from this list for use with a particular implementation of R/3 to satisfy the business requirements. This selection process reflects the business process reengineering that is carried out during configuration. The BPP Master List is keyed to the R/3 System business processes by the procedure title (Level 6, **Figure 10.3**) and the R/3 transaction code

FIGURE 10.4
BPP Master List
Cross-References

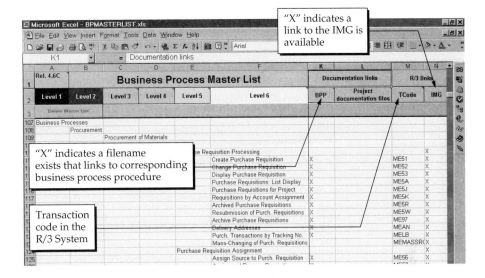

FIGURE 10.5
In-Scope Processes
for BPP Master List

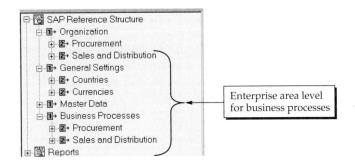

(TCode, **Figure 10.4**). These are grouped by application module or enterprise area with some overlap where a specific process is used within more than one application area. If a particular module is not being implemented, those processes are readily skipped. The implementation team selects the process scenarios in the SAP Reference Structure as "in scope" (**Figure 10.5**) for a company's particular implementation. The hierarchy of the SAP Reference Structure corresponds to the levels in the BPP Master List. The selected in-scope processes are based on the business requirements for the R/3 System implementation and are used to generate the BPP Master List that contains only the in-scope process procedures. This Master List is also keyed to "standard" accelerator documents that can be used to gather the necessary information for configuring and documenting a selected R/3 System process (**Figure 10.3**). The BPP Master List contains a BPP documentation link, which is the unique identifier for the Business Process Procedure ID in ASAP. The Level 6 column contains the name for this process or procedure. The TCode column of the R/3 link identifies the specific transaction code of the process procedure that is to be included in the configured system (**Figure 10.4**). Once the process procedures have been configured, end users can test those features of the system and provide feedback for any potential adjustments. These adjustments occur during the Realization phase of the ASAP Roadmap.

The BPP Master List workbook contains several additional worksheets for organizing the tasks required for configuration. Each cycle sheet provides a means for creating a list of business processes configured and validated in that particular cycle. As in other prototyping development, each cycle is a refinement of the previous cycle as the project team works toward the complete implementation. An "X" in the BPP column of the Documentation links (**Figure 10.4**) indicates that an ASAP accelerator document is available for use in configuring that process. The document can be selected and accessed from the BPP Master List and provides guidance in completing the configuration of the process. The ASAP methodology provides a means for selecting those BPPs that are to be included in the configuration. These are selected as **in-scope processes** (**Figure 10.5**). A fundamental activity of configuration is following the ASAP Roadmap in the selection of these in-scope BPPs.

Selected enterprise areas require the activation of master data used by the business processes within that area. For the Level 2 scenarios of Procurement and of Sales and Distribution indicated as in-scope (see **Figure 10.5**), master records are needed for the Material Master, Customer Master Record, and Vendor Master Record. These master records appear at Level 3 in the SAP Reference Structure hierarchy (see **Figure 10.6**).

The lowest level of the SAP Reference Structure is Level 5. When the Level 4 Sales Order process group is selected, the Level 5 processes of Customer Quotation Processing and Sales Order Processing are set in-scope (see **Figure 10.7**). The Sales Order Processing (Standard) scenario, Level 3, includes Sales Order, Shipping, and Billing process groups, but several groups are excluded, for example, Costing and Warehouse Management (**Figure 10.7**), as indicated by not being selected as in-scope. Clearly, having these selections use this SAP Reference Structure is much easier than doing these specifications using only the IMG.

FIGURE 10.6
In-Scope Master Records for BPP Master List at Level 3

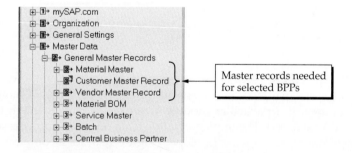

FIGURE 10.7
In-Scope Sales Order Business Process Elements for Sales Order Processing at Level 5

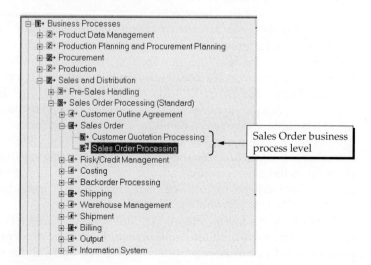

FIGURE 10.8
Master Record BPP
Document

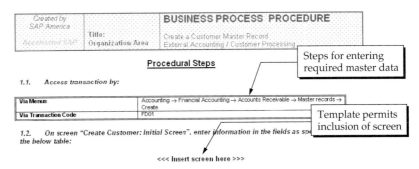

FIGURE 10.9
Number Range BPP
Document

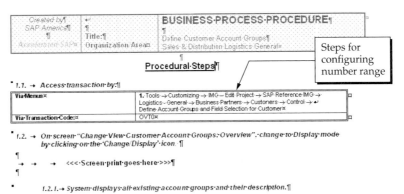

BPP Document

A BPP document is the lowest-level accelerator that is used to collect information about a specific R/3 business process and provides detailed guidance in performing the related configuration activities using the IMG and the Reference Model. A typical BPP document for creating a master record (**Figure 10.8**) is a Microsoft Word document that contains a Procedural Steps section, which includes the menu selections and transaction code for actually carrying out the configuration activity using the data gathered with the particular document. Furthermore, it contains a template layout for providing screen captures and related instructions for performing these activities. The result is documentation that can be used by future team members to provide ongoing maintenance support for the R/3 System installation. About 2,000 of these document templates are provided in the tool kit for the business process procedures.

Another example of an accelerator is a BPP document that is used to establish the detail specification for the customer numbers groups that would be specified in the Define Customer Account Groups BBP document (see **Figure 10.9**). In this manner, information concerning user requirements is gathered to complete the related BPP documents that are then used to carry out the actual configuration of the R/3 System. They document this configuration activity for future reference and use in training.

Reference IMG

The Implementation Guide (IMG) is a component of the SAP R/3 System that provides detailed steps for carrying out the actual configuration settings of the selected application modules. The Reference IMG, introduced previously in

Chapter 7—Configuration, consists of the particular components that are included in the configuration that customizes the R/3 System to meet the processing requirements for a company. The IMG lists all the required actions for implementing the R/3 System and assists in the control and documentation of the implementation.

Activities carried out in the IMG include making global settings and specifying the organizational structure. Then the individual application modules or areas are configured as determined by the business requirements and indicated under the project scope. Examples of global settings are the specification of the countries with which the company does business and establishing the currency table for all these countries. SAP follows the ISO standard, a standard published by the International Organization for Standardization, when establishing the countries and their associated currencies. The activities for doing the country settings, as described in Extended R/3 Help, are as follows:

1. Check that the country entries are complete.
2. Add the missing countries if necessary.
3. Use the ISO standard for your entries.

A similar set of activities is performed for specifying the currencies, which should also follow the ISO standard.

The Reference IMG is where the configuration of the business requirements in the R/3 System is actually done (see **Figure 10.10**). The business requirements determine the enterprise areas and the business processes that are included in the configuration. The detailed configuration parameters are recorded in the BBP document for the selected business processes. Once recorded, these parameters are then entered into the R/3 System using the Reference IMG.

Besides assisting in the configuration of the selected business processes, the IMG facilitates entering the organizational structure for the company. Recall that the definition of organization units is a fundamental step in an R/3 implementation project, because it is such a critical factor in how the relationships among the business units and functions will be arranged. The minimum number of organization units should be used. Once an organizational structure has been established, it is not easy to change it. Using analysis of the business requirements, the

FIGURE 10.10
Role of Reference IMG in Configuration

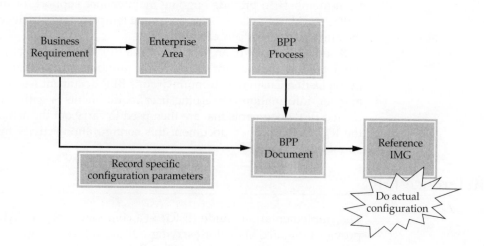

FIGURE 10.11
Reference Structure
Definition Activities
for Financial
Accounting

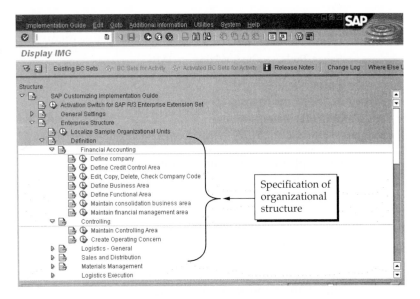

FIGURE 10.12
Reference IMG for
Customer Control
Activities

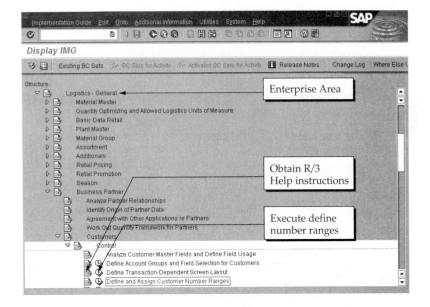

organizational units are specified under the Reference Structure in the IMG (see **Figure 10.11**). This includes establishing the company code, the business area, the sales organization, and the controlling area, as described previously in *Chapter 9— Organization Structure*. The IMG supports defining the Reference Structure as it relates to each of the application areas, such as Financial Accounting, Treasury, Controlling, Logistics—General, and Sales and Distribution.

After establishing this organizational structure, the business processes are configured for the selected enterprise areas. Each area has its specific set of configuration activities. The Define and Assign Customer Number Ranges activity is one of these activities for the Logistics area (see **Figure 10.12**).

The Define and Assign Customer Number Ranges process (**Figure 10.12**) is reached from the SAP Easy Access screen by this menu path:

Select **Tools** → **Customizing** → **IMG** →

   Edit Project → **SAP Reference IMG**

The Display IMG screen appears (**Figure 10.12**).

Select **Logistics – General** → **Business Partner** → **Customers** →

   Control → **Define and Assign Customer Number Ranges**

An example of a menu path for this kind of configuration activity is shown under the Procedural Steps section in the Number Range BPP document (shown previously in **Figure 10.9**). This is available as an ASAP accelerator document listed in the BPP Master List. So, once the data describing the business requirements for this process is recorded using the accelerator document, that document can be used to perform the actual configuration activity. During this procedure if further explanation of the Define and Assign Customer Number Range process is necessary to help understand this activity, additional instructions (see **Figure 10.13**) can be obtained from the R/3 Online Help. This Online Help is requested from the Display IMG: Define and Assign Customer Number Ranges Online Help icon as indicated in **Figure 10.12**.

The number ranges are displayed for either review (Display Interval button) or change (Change Interval button) from the Customer Number Ranges screen. That screen displays when the Define and Assign Customer Number Ranges option is selected. The Maintain Number Range Intervals screen (**Figure 10.14**) displays the

FIGURE 10.13
Define and Assign Customer Number Ranges from R/3 Help Performance Assistant

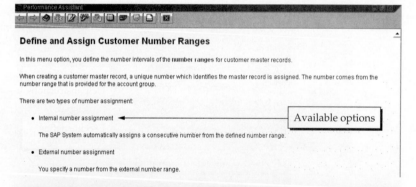

FIGURE 10.14
Maintain Number Range Intervals in IMG

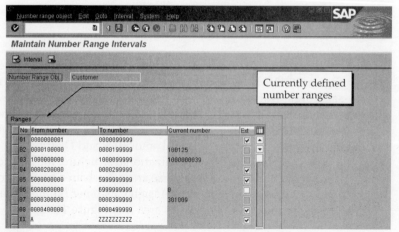

existing number ranges, which are ready for change as appropriate. During the early stages of configuration an existing number range may display on this screen as a result of using a preconfigured client, so this configuration activity may be one to either revise the existing range or add another range.

When a configuration activity such as Define and Assign Customer Number Ranges is completed, another process in the Enterprise Area is selected for configuration from the BBP Master List for the current Cycle; the procedure repeats for the configuration of this next process. With several project teams assigned to different Enterprise Areas, the configuration in those areas may take place concurrently to expedite the overall R/3 System configuration. Once the configuration activities such as this have been completed as indicated in the BPP Master List, the R/3 System is ready for testing by the end users. During the Realization phase of the ASAP Roadmap a number of configuration and testing cycles occur as a completed configuration is prepared. Then a company is ready for the Final Preparation and Go Live phases. The result is an SAP R/3 Enterprise system that is placed into production. It begins handling the day-to-day transaction process actions with this installed system. That processing continues until the R/3 Enterprise system is ready for an upgrade.

Quick Check

1. True or false: The Solution Manager Tool Kit helps consultants use the IMG and SAP Reference Structure during configuration.

2. A(n) _____ is some type of document that is useful in collecting data or managing the project for carrying out configuration tasks.

3. A(n) _____ process is one that has been selected for inclusion in a company's configuration of the R/3 System.

4. The BPML is organized in _____ to support the prototyping refinements that occur during a typical configuration.

5. The _____ column of the BPML indicates the availability of an SAP supporting document.

6. The BPML is used to select the processes in the _____ that will be used for the current implementation to meet a particular business requirement.

7. True or false: The BPP documents accessed from the BPML frequently contain the procedural steps for configuring the related R/3 process.

8. The _____ standard is used when establishing codes for the countries and their associated currencies during configuration.

9. The _____ R/3 screen is used to define and assign customer number ranges.

10. True or false: R/3 supports the use of only one unique customer number range interval.

Displaying SAP R/3 Information

Part 2

11

Exploring System Capabilities

You can display SAP R/3 Enterprise System information that resides in the R/3 application database for review and use. Besides displaying data for individual transactions, you can use the Executive Information Systems (EIS) feature of R/3 to display summarized information. Frequently, you need to look up information in response to an inquiry by a customer or a business partner. Displaying this information is readily performed within the R/3 System. Examples of transaction data that you can display are the content of a customer sales order or the material of a product.

Motor Sports International (MSI) is used to illustrate the operation of the R/3 System. Data for this example company resides in the R/3 System, and it is configured with the business processes necessary to carry out their supply chain processing activities. The North American Training Database of the International Demonstration and Training System (IDES) contains the MSI data that you can access in displaying R/3 information.

Displaying transaction data and information from the R/3 Systems provides a means for you to experience the use of menus, matchcodes, and report trees in navigating the R/3 System. This also introduces you to the complexities that occur in processing business transactions. Because the R/3 System usually provides multiple menu paths for specifying a command, the menu selections shown represent only one of the available methods for invoking the desired command. Also, for more experienced users, transaction codes can be used to directly access an R/3 screen and bypass the menu selections. As you become more experienced with R/3, you may use any of the menu paths or the transaction codes. The important point is that you can access the screen, which contains the information that you want to view, enter, or revise. In this section you will display customer data for a sales order and material data for a product. You will also view summary information as predefined reports from the controlling (CO) application module and from the Executive Information System. Before you display R/3 information, you need to log onto the system.

Logging Onto R/3

Before you can use the R/3 system, you need to log on. When you are done working on your tasks in the R/3 system, you log off. The SAP R/3 logon process asks you to specify a client, to give your user name and password, and to select the language used in displaying the R/3 screens and menus. The **client** is the data set that you use within the R/3 database and must be specified for accessing the appropriate MSI data from the training database. Also, if you want to work in a language other than English, you need to see your system administrator or instructor to make sure you know the language key for your desired language.

The first time you log on, and at regular intervals thereafter, you should change your password. Your R/3 System administrator may assign you a unique user name and password with an initial password to use when you log on for the first time. If you have a unique logon, then during the process of logging on, you should give yourself a new password, one that you create. After that, you use your own password whenever you log on. In the steps that follow, you are instructed to use the mouse pointer in selecting each field. The R/3 System also allows you to press the Tab key after you enter data in a field. When you press the Tab key, the cursor moves to the beginning of the next field.

You need to use the client number that contains the data for the North American Training Database, which has the data that you will display. Before you log on, make sure you know your client number, user name, and password.

To log onto the R/3 System:

1. Click the **start** button on the Taskbar, point to **Programs,** point to **SAP Frontend,** and then click **SAPlogon** to display the SAP Logon screen. Highlight the server assigned by your professor and click **Logon.** This will bring you to the SAP R/3 logon screen. (See **Figure 11.1.**)

Trouble?   The menu path and selections may be different for your R/3 installation. Look for similar menu choices. If you cannot find the menu item to launch R/3, see your instructor or technical support person.

2. Click the **Client** text box, delete the value displayed in this text box, and then type your client number.
3. Click the **User** text box and type your user name.
4. Click the **Password** text box and then type your password. If you are prompted to change your password, type your new password as requested.

FIGURE 11.1
SAP R/3 Logon
Screen

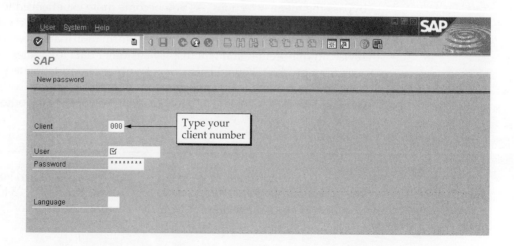

5. Click the **Language** text box, and then type **EN** to specify English; if you are using a different language, type the letter for that language.

6. Click the **Enter** button ✅ to display the Copyright dialog box, and then press the **Enter** key to display the SAP R/3 Easy Access menu screen.

You are now logged onto the SAP R/3 Enterprise System and are ready to display transaction information from the SAP R/3 database.

Caution!   The data shown in the screens that you display may be different than the data shown in the various figures in this section. The figures have been generated using a fresh copy of the IDES training data. If the *fields* displayed on the screen are the same, you have the correct screen. Check with your instructor or technical support person regarding differences that may have occurred in your IDES training data.

Displaying a Sales Order

The sales order is the central document in Sales and Distribution used with Customer Order Management processing. During order entry, information on the customer and products or services is recorded in this document. Information in the sales order is transferred to subsequent documents, which are used in carrying out the processing of the business transaction. Once a sales order has been entered in the R/3 system, you can display it later to review its contents. This might occur in response to a customer inquiry concerning an order. A previously created sales order can be accessed for display either (1) by using a sales order number assigned by the R/3 System when the order was created or (2) by using the customer's purchase order number. The sales order number used in the R/3 system is a unique number, whereas a customer's purchase order number may not be unique. Lyndsay Applewood from Cycle Concepts in Valley Forge, Pennsylvania, contacts you at MSI to inquire about the order quantity of a recently placed order.

To view an existing sales order:

1. Click the **Logistics** expand button ▷ on the SAP Easy Access menu. This is known as expanding the Easy Access menu. You can expand an Easy Access menu item by clicking the expand button or by double-clicking the menu name, for example, Logistics. Now expand **Sales/Distribution** and expand **Sales** to display the Sales menu. (See **Figure 11.2.**)

2. Expand **Order** on the Sales menu, and then double-click **Display** to view the Display Sales Order: Initial Screen. (See **Figure 11.3.**) If a list arrow appears adjacent to the Order text box, this indicates a list is available that could be used for selecting a value for this text box. However, this screen includes the Search Criteria section, where you can enter values directly without opening a separate dialog box, and this is the feature that is used here to find the customer's purchase order information.

3. In the Search Criteria section, click anywhere in the **Purchase Order No.** text box to activate it; then type **CC-76653,** which is the customer's purchase order number that Lyndsay gave you. You need to look up the unique MSI number that is assigned by the R/3 System as the sales order was created, and the selection criteria enable you to do that.

FIGURE 11.2
Menu Path to
Display Sales Order

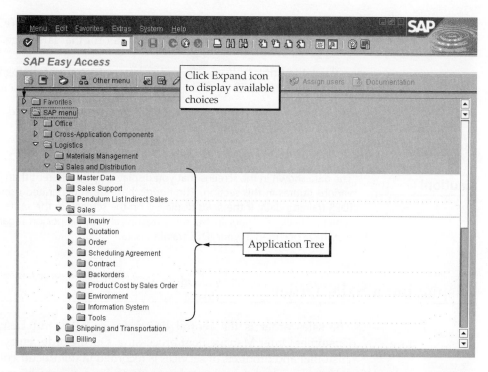

FIGURE 11.3
Display Sales
Order: Initial
Screen

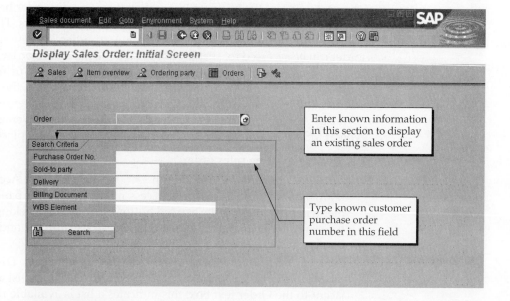

4. Click the **Search** button at the bottom-left corner of the Search Criteria section to display the customer purchase order number. (See **Figure 11.4.**)

5. Double-click anywhere on the value **CC-76653** to display the Standard Order screen. (See **Figure 11.5.**)

Trouble?

The data displayed for your sales order may be different. If the *fields* displayed on the screen are the same, you have the correct screen. Continue by answering the questions for this step.

FIGURE 11.4
Choose Desired
Sales Order Using
Customer Purchase
Order Number

Purchase order ...	SOr...	Sold-to ...	DChl	Dv	SOff.	SGrp	Created ...	SaTy	PO date	TrG	Document	Item
CC-76653	1000	1300	12	00	1010	111	CURA	OR	28.01.1997	0	5013	000000

Restrict Value Range (1) 1 Entry found

Select order

FIGURE 11.5
Standard Order
Screen

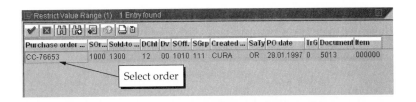

Display Standard Order 5013: Overview

Selected order

Standard Order	5013	Net value 667.700,00 DEM
Sold-to party	1300	Christal Clear / An der Breiten Wiese 122 / 30625 Hannover
Ship-to party	1300	Christal Clear / An der Breiten Wiese 122 / 30625 Hannover
PO Number	CC-76653	PO date 28.01.1997

Sales | Item overview | Item detail | Ordering party | Procurement | Shipping | Reason for rejection

Req. deliv.date	D	30.01.1997	Deliver.Plant	
Complete dlv.			Total Weight	9.600 KG
Delivery block			Volume	192 M3
Billing block			Pricing date	28.01.1997
Payment card			Exp.date	
Payment terms	ZB01	14 Days 3%, 30/2..	Incoterms	CPT Hannover
Order reason				
Sales area	1000 / 12 / 00	Germany Frankfurt, Sold for resale, Cross-division		

All items

Item	Material	Order quantity	SU	Description	S	Customer Material Numb	ItCa	DG
10	L-60C	500	CAR	Gluehlampe 60 Watt k..			TAN	
20	L-60Y	30	CAR	Gluehlampe 60 Watt g..			TAN	

Review the Standard order.

What is the MSI Order number? (Standard Order) _____

Review the information in the All items section for your sales order. For the first (topmost) item listed what is the:

Material number (part number) ordered? _____

Order quantity? _____

6. Click the **Sold-to Party** button on the Application toolbar to display additional data for the selected sales order.

What is the name of the company? _____

Next you decide to check the MSI sales order number for your reference by redisplaying the Sales Order: Initial Screen. This shows you how a previously entered value is carried forward for continued use in processing a transaction or in locating other R/3 data.

7. Click the **Cancel** button twice to return to the SAP Easy Access menu, and then double-click **Display** to redisplay the Sales Order: Initial Screen.

Review the Sales Order.

What is the MSI sales order number used by the R/3 system? _____

Is this the same order number as the one displayed on the Standard Order: Overview Screen? _____

Notice that the R/3 System "remembers" the most recent sales order number in the event you want to continue working with this order. Now you are ready to return to the SAP R/3 main menu screen.

8. Click the **Cancel** button [icon] to return to the SAP Easy Access menu.

You have reviewed Lyndsay's sales order and confirmed that the desired quantities and materials were ordered.

Displaying Product Information

In sales and distribution, products are sold or sent to business partners. Master data about the products is the basis for processing business transactions in sales and distribution. In the SAP R/3 System, business transactions are stored in the form of documents. These sales and distribution documents are structured according to certain criteria, with all necessary information stored in a systematic way. In addition to sales and distribution, other departments of the company such as accounting or materials management access the master data. If you need an overview of a product or want to check a material master record, you can display it. However, you *cannot* carry out any changes from the display mode. The material master data, which describes each product, is stored to allow access from the different user views and therefore must meet a wide variety of requirements. For example, during sales processing, the system repeatedly accesses the material master records in the inquiry, in the quotation, and in the sales order. In addition, data in the material master record is important for shipping and billing. However, the data required for shipping is not the same as the data required for sales or billing. For sales and distribution, the general data and the sales and distribution data in the material master record are most relevant.

> **General Data.** General data in a material master record is identical for every sales organization, plant, and storage location. General data, which is important for all departments, is always entered by the department that creates the first part or view of the master record. Examples of General data contents are the material number that identifies it, the material description, units of measure, value, weight, volume, and divisions.

> **Sales and Distribution Data.** Sales and distribution data in a material master record is defined for a specific sales organization and distribution channel. Examples of sales and distribution data are the delivery plant, the assignment to the sales group, grouping terms for price agreements, and sales texts. The fact that a material is linked to a distribution channel allows the material to be sold with different conditions through the various distribution channels.

You can find the master data for a particular product by using Search Help, previously known as matchcodes. **Search Help** is an R/3 query tool you use to find specific information for field values used in completing transactions. Search Help takes partial values you input to search for data such as material or part name, a customer or supplier name, a city, or a description.

Tom Burnside, from Overland Trucking, phones you to ask for the standard price of an MSI 350 CC motorcycle. You need to look up the price for him by displaying product information.

To display master data about a product:

1. Expand **Logistics** on the SAP Easy Access menu, expand **Sales and Distribution,** expand **Master Data,** and then expand **Products.** Next expand the

Material menu; then expand **Trading Goods.** (See **Figure 11.6.**) Create, Change, and Display are common activities used with many of the R/3 System transactions, such as the Trading Goods transaction.

2. Double-click **Display** to bring up the Display Material: Initial Screen. (See **Figure 11.7.**) Notice the Search Help list button 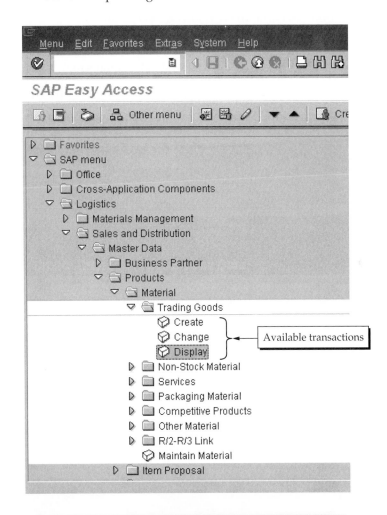 to the right of the Material text box, which indicates a list is available that can be used to display the Search Help dialog box to find the desired value in this user input text box.

FIGURE 11.6
Menu Path to
Display Material:
Initial Screen

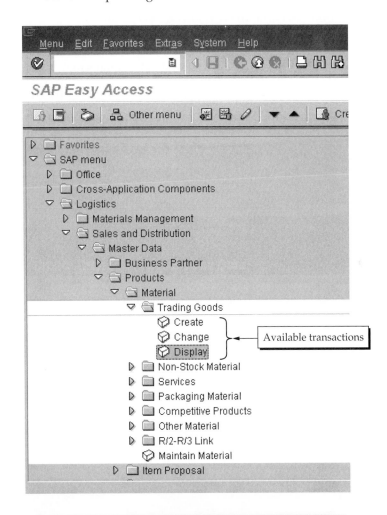

FIGURE 11.7
Display Material:
Initial Screen

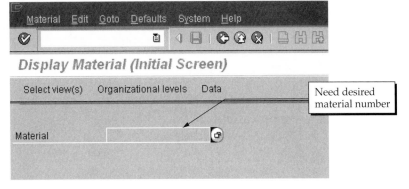

Trouble?

If a value appears in the Material text box, it is because this value was selected previously. This is not an error, but represents different actions within a screen.

3. Click the **Material** text box to activate it and to display its Search Help list button ⬚. Click the **Material Search Help** list button to open the Search Help selection dialog box. (See **Figure 11.8**.)

4. In the **Material description** text box, type ***CYCLE*** as the text string you want to find. The asterisk (*) acts as a wildcard character. This value gives you a list of any material descriptions that contain the text string "CYCLE". Click the **Start search** button ✅ or press the **Enter** key. (See **Figure 11.9**.)

5. Click anywhere on the Material value **1400-510** to choose that material for the 350 motorcycle, and then click the **Enter** button ✅ to return to the Display Material: Initial Screen with the selected material number.

FIGURE 11.8
Search Help
Selection Dialog
Box

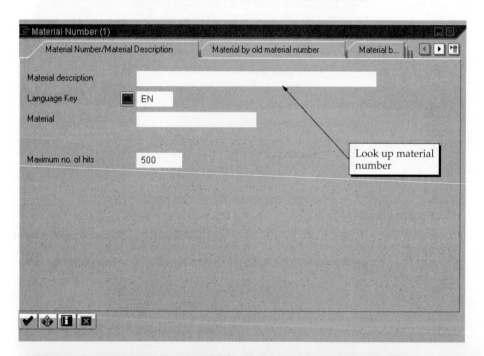

FIGURE 11.9
Search Result List
Dialog Box

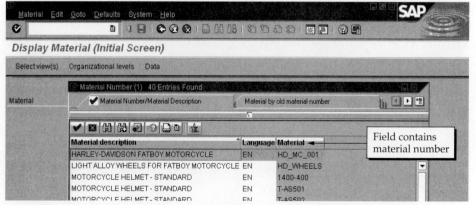

Trouble? If your cursor remains an hourglass, click anywhere on the Material number to change the pointer back to an arrow.

Trouble? If the above Material number is not available for your transaction data, see your instructor for a different Material number and repeat step 5.

6. Click the **Select view(s)** button **Select view(s)** on the Application toolbar to display the Select View(s) dialog box. (See **Figure 11.10.**) Each view consists of different data from the R/3 database.

7. Click the **Select all** button to choose all the available data views; then click the **Enter** button to display the Organization Levels dialog box. (See **Figure 11.11.**)

FIGURE 11.10
Select View(s)
Dialog Box

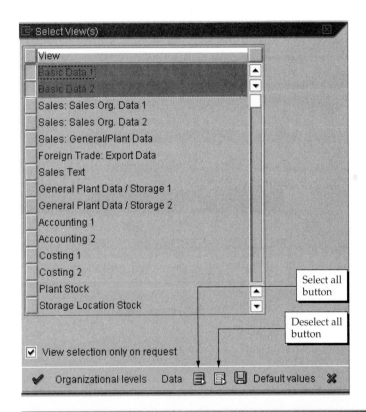

FIGURE 11.11
Organization Levels
Dialog Box

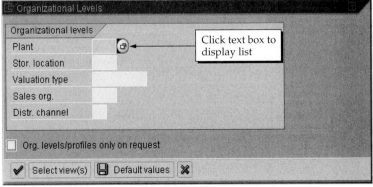

8. Click the **Plant** text box to activate it, and then click the **Plant Search Help** list button to display the Possible Entries: Plants dialog box for selecting the matchcode. (See **Figure 11.12.**)

9. Double-click anywhere on the value **3000** to choose the plant number, and return to the Organizational Levels dialog box.

10. Click the **Continue** (**Enter**) button 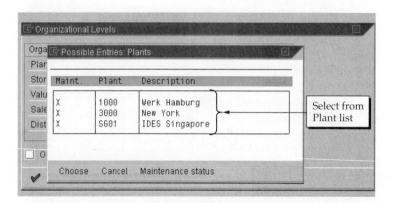 to view the Display Material 1400-510 (Finished product) screen. (See **Figure 11.13.**)

11. Click the different tabs to display the various data, such as sales organization data, and the general/plant data.

    Review the data in the Basic data 1 section.

    What is the standard price of this cycle? (Hint: Accounting 1 screen)

    _____

You are now ready to return to the SAP Easy Access screen.

FIGURE 11.12
Possible Entries:
Plant Dialog Box

FIGURE 11.13
Display Material
Basic Data Screen

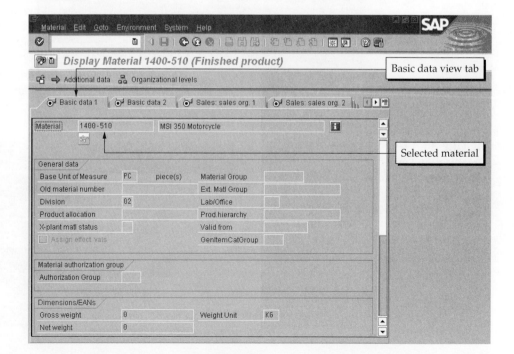

12. Click the **Exit** button ⟦🏠⟧ on the Standard toolbar to return to the SAP Easy Access menu.

You have now verified the standard price of the MSI 350 Motorcycle for Tom at the Overland Trucking Company.

Producing a Cost Center Report

Cost Center Accounting is used to determine where costs occur in the organization based on a specified cost center as an activity within Financial Module processing. The **cost center** is an organizational unit in a controlling area representing a clearly defined or delimited location where costs occurred. Costs are assigned to those organizational subareas where the costs occurred and where they may be influenced. This assignment of costs not only makes cost control possible, but it also provides vital specifications for the other subcategories in the SAP R/3 System's cost accounting applications.

Cost centers are used for differentiated assignment of overhead costs to sales activities (cost calculation functions) and for carrying out differentiated controlling of costs occurring in an organization (cost controlling function). That is, a **cost center** is an organizational unit where you want to keep track of various business expenses. Before you can create cost centers, you must define a cost center hierarchy. This is referred to in CO-CCA as a standard hierarchy. The standard hierarchy is directly assigned to the controlling area during SAP R/3 System configuration. Each time you create a cost center, you must assign it to a cost center group within the standard hierarchy. This ensures that all the cost centers within a particular controlling area are grouped together. When analyzing the standard hierarchy, the system automatically includes all cost centers.

The cost center structure ideally reflects the organizational structure of your company. It remains constant over long periods and provides a framework in which cost center planning is carried out. You can create periodic reports for both cost centers and cost center groups, which can be submitted to the relevant managers for analysis. These reports can help to identify economic weaknesses and planning errors in individual cost centers.

The **report tree** can assist you in selecting cost center reports from the information system. It is a freely definable structure that you can access from within any application. The report tree gathers all reports within an application and sorts them by hierarchy. You access reports by selecting end nodes from the report tree.

MSI has several reporting requirements for different areas in the company. Different management levels are interested in reporting on profitability, profit centers, cost centers, and internal orders. Reports for these different areas are available as a report tree for selecting the desired report.

Sam Wyman from the Human Resources department stops by your office to discuss costs in his department, which belongs to the Finance and Administration business unit. During your discussion, Sam asks you to display the Actual/Plan/Variance report for his department so you can review the Salaries—Base Wages of the department.

To produce a cost center report:

1. If the Logistics menu is open, click the **Collapse** button ⟦▽⟧ to close that menu. This collapsing of the open menu is best done in order to limit your displayed SAP Easy Access menu.

2. Now expand **Accounting** on the SAP Easy Access menu, expand **Controlling**, and then expand **Cost Center Accounting.** Next expand **Information System,** expand **Reports for Cost Center Accounting,** and then expand the **Plan/Actual Comparisons** menu to display the list of available reports. (See **Figure 11.14.**)

3. Double-click anywhere on **Cost Centers: Actual/Plan/Variance** to select that cost center report and to display the Cost Centers: Actual/plan/variance: Selection screen. (See **Figure 11.15.**)

Trouble?

If the Set Controlling Area dialog box displays, type **2000** in the **Controlling area** text box; then click the **Continue** button.

FIGURE 11.14
Expanded
Application Tree

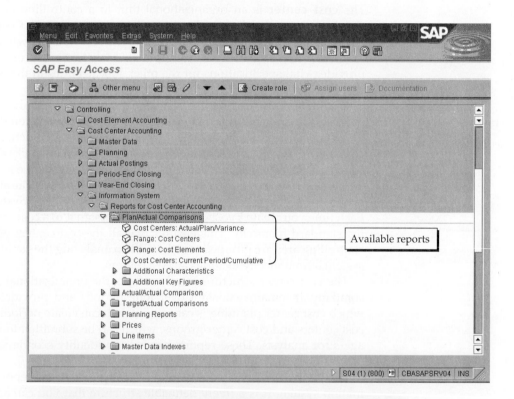

FIGURE 11.15
Cost Centers:
Actual/Plan/
Variance: Selection
Screen

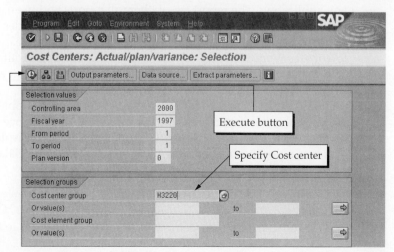

FIGURE 11.16
Human Resources
Cost Center Report

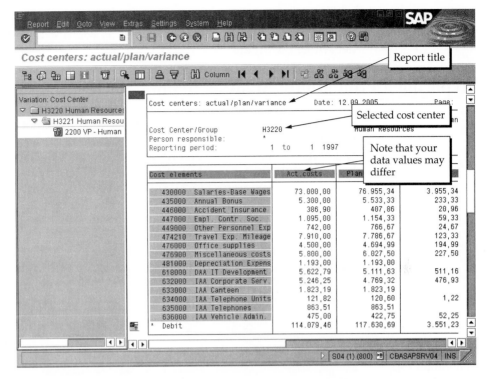

4. In the Selection values section, type **2000** in the **Controlling area** text box. Type **1997** in the **Fiscal year** text box, and then type **1** in the **To period** text box.

5. In the Selection groups section, click the **Search Help** button for the Cost center group to display the Cost center group dialog box. Type **2000** in the **Controlling area** text box, and then click the **Proceed (Enter)** button to select the Cost center group. Scroll the list as needed until the value H3220 appears; then double-click the value **H3220** to complete the selections in this dialog box. Of course, you could also have used Search Help to select the cost center.

6. Click the **Execute** button on the Application toolbar to produce the cost center report. (See **Figure 11.16.**)

Trouble?

If the Select: Extracts screen appears, telling you that there are already reports stored as extracts for the criteria you entered, it just means that this report has been run previously and has been saved. Ask your instructor which extracts you are to display.

Review the report.

What is the actual cost for Salaries—Base Wages? _____

Now you can return to the SAP R/3 main menu screen for your next processing activity.

7. Click the **Exit** button to display the Exit report dialog box, and then click the **Yes** button to return to the Cost Center: Actual/plan/variance: Selection menu, click the **Exit** button to return to the SAP Easy Access menu, and then collapse the **Accounting** menu to close it.

You have displayed the Human Resources cost center report and found the total salaries—base wages for that cost center as you discussed the operation of that department with Sam.

Preparing a Profitability Analysis Report

Profitability Analysis (CO-PA) is a Financial module activity that lets you evaluate market segments or strategic business units such as company codes. A **market segment** is a classification according to products, customers, orders, or any combination of these. A **company code** is used to classify the business areas of the profit centers with respect to a company's profit or contribution margin. The aim of the CO-PA system is to provide your sales, marketing, product management, and corporate planning departments with information to support internal accounting and decision making.

CO-PA can be implemented in companies in any branch of industry (mechanical engineering, wholesale and retail, chemical, service industries, and so on) and with any form of production (repetitive manufacturing, make-to-order manufacturing, process manufacturing). The data can be displayed by period or arranged

FIGURE 11.17
Application Tree for Profitability Analysis Report

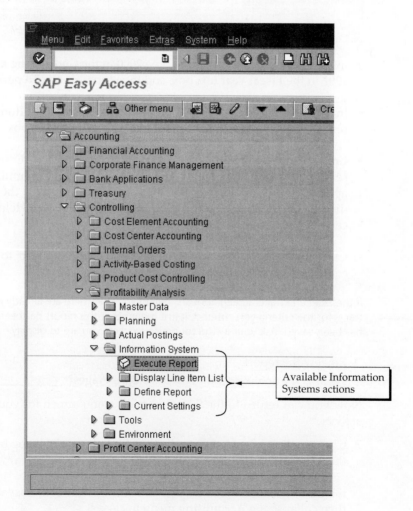

by order or project. This allows you to analyze profitability by comparing costs and revenues. You have a meeting scheduled with Robin Stressman in the Product Development department to review the profitability of MSI's different motorcycle product lines. This information is available in a profitability analysis report. You want to review the profitability of the 2500 CC motorcycle before you meet with Robin.

To prepare a profitability analysis report:

1. Expand **Accounting** on the SAP Easy Access menu, expand **Controlling,** expand **Profitability Analysis,** and expand **Information system.** (See **Figure 11.17.**)

2. Double-click **Execute Report** to display the Set Operating Concern dialog box.

   If it does not display, click the **Execute report** button 🕒 to open the Set Operating Concern dialog box. (See **Figure 11.18.**)

3. Click the **Operating concern Search Help** list button 🔳 to display the list of defined operating concerns. (See **Figure 11.19.**)

4. Click anywhere on **IDEA** to select it as the desired operating concern; then click the **Copy** button ☑ of the Operating Concern dialog box. This will return you to the Set Operating Concern dialog box. Now click the **Continue (Enter)** button ☑ to open the Run Profitability Report: Initial Screen.

5. Click Report **IDES-011 Daily Contribution Margin Analysis** to select it, and then click the **Execute** button 🕒 on the Application toolbar to open the Selection dialog box. (See **Figure 11.20.**)

FIGURE 11.18
Set Operating
Concern Dialog Box

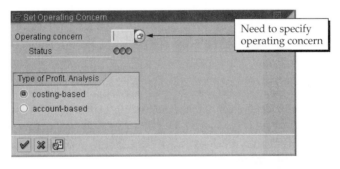

FIGURE 11.19
Operating Concern
Dialog Box

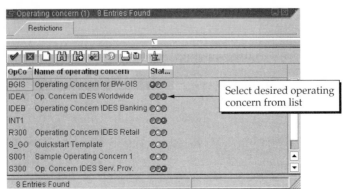

FIGURE 11.20
Selection: Daily
Contribution
Margin Analysis
Report Screen

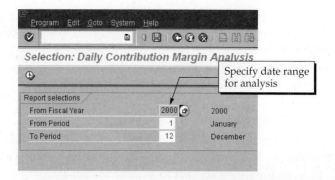

FIGURE 11.21
Daily Contribution
Margin Analysis
Report

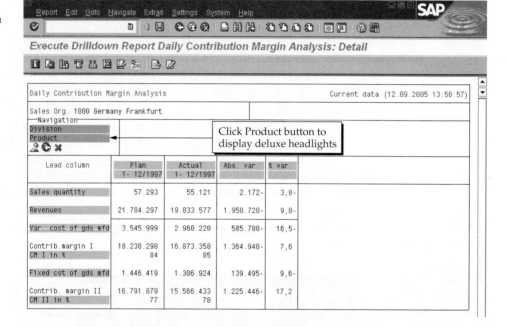

6. Type **1997** in the **From Fiscal Year** box, **1** in the **From Period** box, and **12** in the

   To Period box. Then click the **Execute** button to display the contribution margin report. (See **Figure 11.21.**)

7. Click the **Product** button under the Navigation section to display the Deluxe Headlight screen.

   Review the report.

Trouble?

If the "Drill-Down: Callup for documentation on hotspots" screen appears, you have not previously used the drill-down function. If you want to read more about the hotspots, follow the directions on the screen. To keep from having this screen appear again, click the **Never display again** button.

What is the actual revenue of the deluxe headlight in 1997? _____

You are now ready to return to the SAP R/3 main menu for additional processing activities.

8. Click the **Exit** button on the Standard toolbar to open the Exit Report dialog box, click the **Yes** button to return to the Run Profitability Report: Initial

Screen, click the **Exit** button 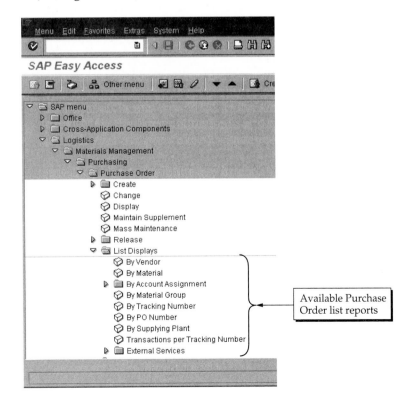 to return to the SAP R/3 menu, and then collapse the **Controlling** menu and the **Accounting** menu.

You have produced the desired profitability analysis report and reviewed the profitability of deluxe headlights in preparation for meeting with Robin.

Creating a Purchase Order List

Motor Sports International (MSI) routinely reviews all areas of its organization's operations to identify opportunities to reduce costs and improve efficiency as part of its procurement processing. MSI reviews historical information to evaluate proposals, estimate costs for product development, and to plan future production. Functional areas are responsible for regularly reviewing their transactions and activities.

MSI must have access to purchasing information for their procurement processing to process material requests from all areas of the company and to respond to vendor inquiries. MSI frequently reviews the status of purchase transactions or purchase orders to determine the last date a material was requisitioned, ordered, received, or invoiced. MSI also reviews the inventory history of a material to verify when and how it was used. Lori Cooper wants you to examine her purchase orders. She wants you to use a purchase order list to review the purchase orders that are currently outstanding at Plant 3000.

To create a purchase order list for a purchasing group by using a variant:

1. Expand **Logistics** on the SAP Easy Access menu, expand **Materials management,** and then expand **Purchasing** to display the Purchasing menu. Expand **Purchase Order** on the Purchasing menu and finally, expand **List Displays.** (See **Figure 11.22.**)

FIGURE 11.22
Purchasing Order List Application Tree

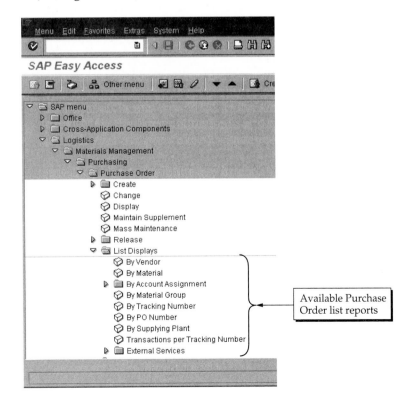

FIGURE 11.23
Purchasing
Documents Per
Vendor
Specification Screen

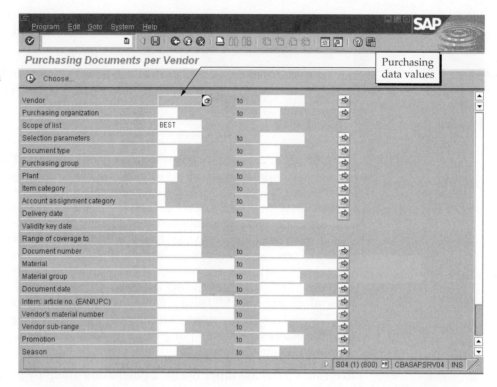

2. Next double-click **By Vendor** to display the Purchasing Documents per Vendor screen for specifying the criteria for the Purchase Order list. (See **Figure 11.23.**)

3. Type **3000** in the **Purchasing organization** text box, type **010** in the **Purchasing group** text box, type **3200** in the **Plant** text box, and then click the **Execute** button to display the Purchasing Documents per Vendor list screen. (See **Figure 11.24.**)

4. Click anywhere on the PO number **4500005014** to select the PO document; then click the **Display document** button on the Application toolbar to display the details of the Purchase Order document. (See **Figure 11.25.**)

Trouble?

If the above purchase order document number is not available, see your instructor for a different document number.

Trouble?

If the PO screen does not show the desired information, you may have to expand the **Header** details and then click the **Item overview** expand button. It depends how this screen was previously accessed. SAP R/3 "remembers" your selections for the last display of this screen and uses those same settings.

Trouble?

If the navigation pane appears and you want to close this pane, click the **Close** button in the navigation pane to display the Standard PO in a full pane. The Item overview may appear without Help in the navigation pane.

FIGURE 11.24
Purchasing
Documents Per
Vendor List Screen

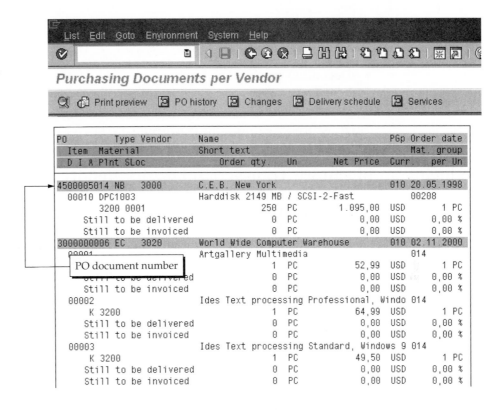

FIGURE 11.25
Display Purchase
Order: Item
Overview Screen

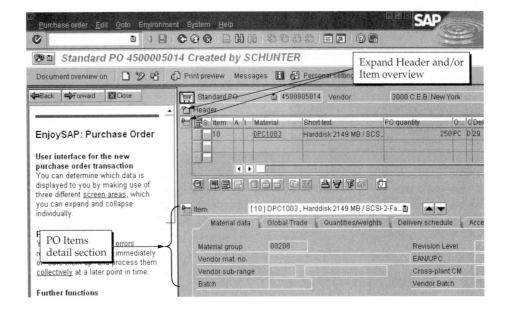

Review the purchase order document.

What is the Short text for this PO item? _____

What is the PO quantity for this item? _____

You now return to the SAP Easy Access menu screen.

5. Click the **Exit** button 🏠 on the Standard toolbar to return to the Purchasing Documents per Vendor list screen, click the **Exit** button 🏠 to return to the SAP Easy Access menu, and then collapse the **Purchasing** menu.

Using a purchase order list, you have reviewed Lori's purchase orders for Plant 3000 and have confirmed the PO quantity for this order.

Producing an Inventory Transaction History Report

In procurement processing, the *Material documents for a material* function displays a list of the material documents posted for one or more materials. A **document** is a record of a business transaction in the R/3 System. The document remains as a complete unit and can be displayed at any time until it is archived. From a material document list, you can select a material document for display.

In the Inventory Management system the physical stocks reflect all transactions resulting in a change in stock and thus in updated inventory levels. You can easily obtain an overview of the current stocks of any given material by reviewing inventory transaction summaries and documents.

> **Document Principle.** In the R/3 inventory management system, the accepted accounting principle of *no posting without a document* applies. According to the document principle, a document must be generated and stored in the system for every transaction/event that causes a change in stock.

When posting a goods movement in the SAP System, the following documents are created:

- **Material document** In the Inventory Management system, when a goods movement is posted, a material document is generated that serves as proof of the movement and as a source of information for any applications that follow. A material document consists of a header and at least one item. The header contains general data about the movement (for example, its date). Each item describes one movement.
- **Accounting document** If the movement is relevant for Financial Accounting (that is, if it leads to an update of the G/L accounts), an accounting document is created parallel to the material document. In some cases, several accounting documents are created for a single material document. An example of such a situation would be when you have two material document items with different plants that belong to different company codes.

> **Document Numbers.** A document number and the material document year identify a material document. The company code, the document number, and the fiscal year identify an accounting document. Usually, the material document number and the accounting document number are different.

Melissa Stevens wants you to use an inventory history report to review the material documents for Plant 3000.

To create an inventory transaction history report:

1. Expand **Logistics** on the SAP Easy Access menu, expand **Materials management,** and then expand **Inventory Management** to display the Inventory Management menu.

FIGURE 11.26
Inventory
Management
Transaction Report
Application Tree

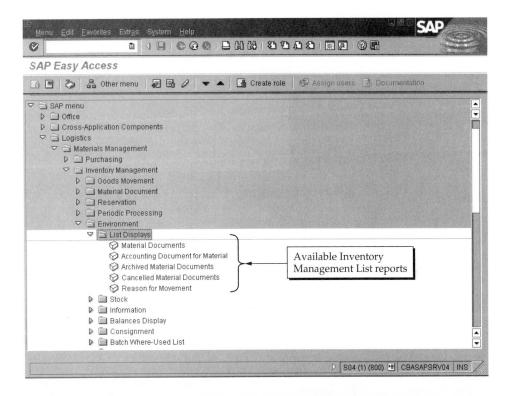

FIGURE 11.27
Display Material
Document List
Screen

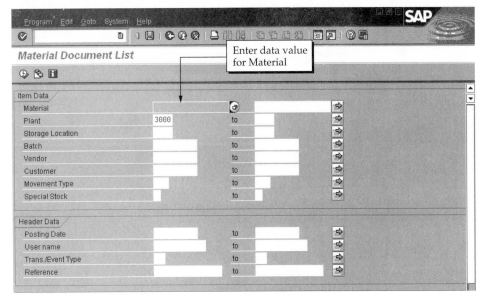

2. Expand **Environment** in the Inventory Management menu, and expand **List Displays** to see a list of available report documents. (See **Figure 11.26.**)

3. Double-click **Material Documents** to view the Material Document List screen. (See **Figure 11.27.**)

Trouble? The last set of previously entered values may appear on this screen. This is not a problem. Just delete any unwanted field values that you want blank, and type over field values that you want to change.

4. Type **1400-510** in the **Material** text box, make sure that the **Plant** number is **3000** and that no other fields are filled, and then click the **Execute** button [image] to display the Material Document List screen. (See **Figure 11.28.**)

5. Click anywhere on the material document number **49002688** to select that material document, and then click the **Choose detail** button [image] on the Application toolbar to perform a drill-down and to display the details of the material document. (See **Figure 11.29.**)

Trouble?

If the above material document number is not available, see your instructor for a different document number.

Review the Material document overview.

What is the amount stored in this storage location for the specified material 1400-510? _____

You are ready to return to the SAP Easy Access menu before you continue with the next processing activity.

FIGURE 11.28
Material Document List by Material Screen

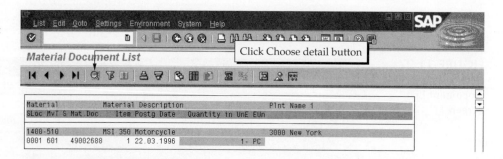

FIGURE 11.29
Display Material Document Overview Screen

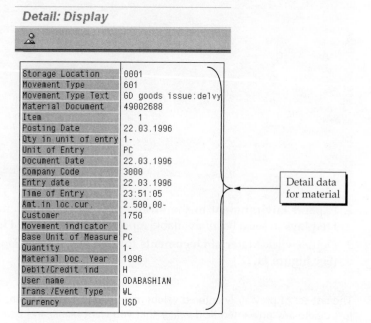

6. Click the **Exit** button on the Standard toolbar to return to the Material Document by Material screen, click the **Exit** button to return to the Inventory Management menu, click the **Exit** button to return to the SAP Easy Access screen, and then collapse the **Materials Management** menu.

You have examined the material document for material 1400-510 at Plant 3000 for Melissa and confirmed the current amount on hand in this material's storage location.

Performing a Material Consumption Analysis

In manufacturing planning and execution processing, MSI must have access to manufacturing information to plan and produce products. In addition to the routine production functions, MSI regularly analyzes its manufacturing patterns to manage production workload and efficiencies, and to identify opportunities for reducing costs.

MSI must be able to determine the latest material plans, production order status, and to verify the availability of work center capacity. They also routinely review the performance of the manufacturing organization: production costs, work center efficiencies, capacity overload conditions, as well as actual versus planned or target lead times for production.

Material Usage. The material usage analysis can be carried out for manufacturing and production orders. By using the material usage analysis, you are able to ask and answer the following questions: What were the total components used for a material? Which components were affected by the material usage? What was the original requirements quantity, and what was actually taken from inventory?

Tom Peters wants you to analyze the material consumption at the New York plant by using a standard analysis.

To prepare a standard analysis of material consumption:

1. If necessary, expand **Logistics** on the SAP Easy Access menu, and then expand **Logistics Controlling,** expand **Shop Floor Information System,** and expand **Standard Analyses.** (See **Figure 11.30.**)
2. Double-click **Material Consumption** to display the Material Usage Analysis: Selection screen. (See **Figure 11.31.**)
3. Type **3000** in the **Plant** text box to specify the desired plant for analysis.
4. Delete the other values in the Characteristics section for the **Material** number and the **Order** number, if they appear. Next delete the date values in the Period to analyze section for the **Date** text boxes; then click the **Execute** button to display the Material Usage Analysis: Basic List. (See **Figure 11.32.**)
5. Double-click anywhere on the **Plant** name **New York** to select that Plant and to perform a drill-down that displays the details of the Material usage. (See **Figure 11.33.**)

FIGURE 11.30
Material
Consumption
Application Tree

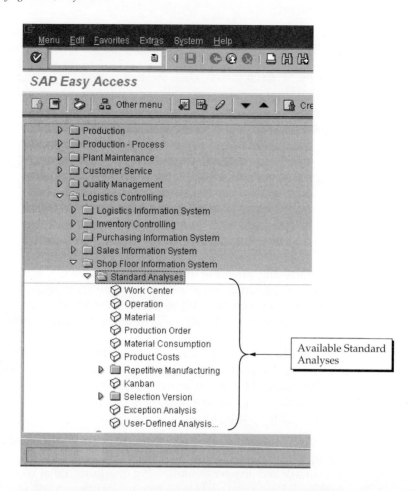

FIGURE 11.31
Material Usage
Analysis: Selection
Screen

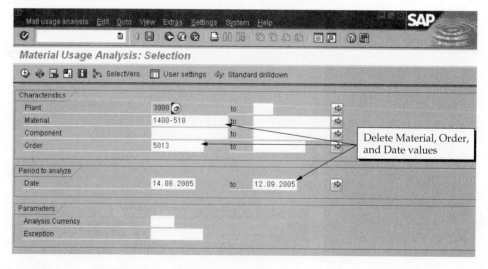

6. Click the **Withdrawal Qty** column heading to select that column, and then click

   the **Top N...** button Top N... on the Application toolbar to open the Top N dialog box.

FIGURE 11.32
Material Usage
Analysis: Basic List
Screen

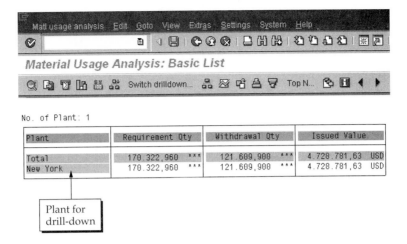

FIGURE 11.33
Material Usage
Analysis: Drilldown
Screen

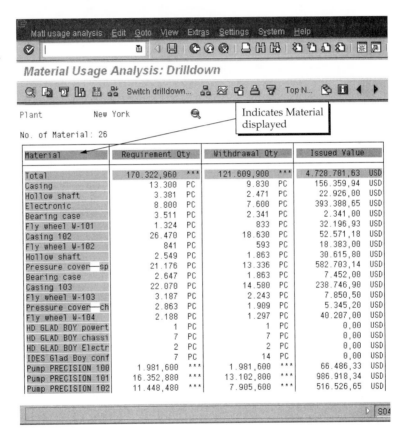

7. Type **4** in the **Number** text box to specify that as the number of items you want
   displayed. Then click the **Continue (Enter)** button ✓ to display a list of the
   largest or Top 4 Withdrawal Qty. (See **Figure 11.34.**)

8. Click the **Switch drilldown...** button Switch drilldown... on the Application toolbar
   to display the Switch drilldown dialog box, click the **Component** option button

FIGURE 11.34
Material Usage Analysis: Ranking List Screen

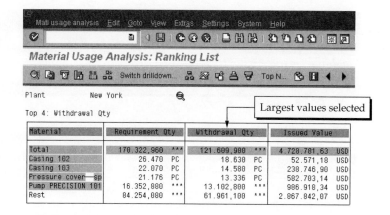

FIGURE 11.35
Material Usage Analysis: Ranking List Screen with Top 4 Components

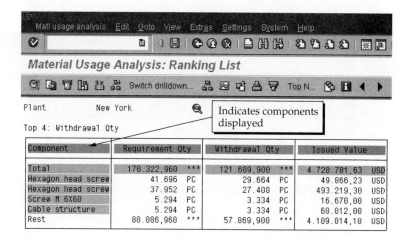

to select that drill-down, and then click the **Continue (Enter)** button [image] to display the Top N Component list. (See **Figure 11.35.**)

Review the Material Usage Analysis.

Which component has the largest quantity withdrawn?

_____

What is that quantity? _____

Now return to the SAP Easy Access menu.

9. Click the **Exit** button [image] on the Standard toolbar to open the Exit Material Usage Analysis dialog box, click the **No** button to return to the Material Usage

Analysis: Selection screen, click the **Exit** button [image] to return to the SAP Easy Access menu, and then collapse the **Logistics Controlling** menu and the **Logistics** menu.

Using a standard analysis for material consumption, you have determined the largest top four materials and components for Tom.

Displaying a Predefined EIS Report

An executive information system provides information about all the factors that influence the business activities of a company. SAP-EIS is an executive information system that is used to collect and evaluate information from different areas of a business and its environment. To achieve this, an individual SAP-EIS database is set up that has data supplied from various subinformation systems such as the financial information system, personnel information system, logistics information system, or cost accounting. As data comes from different areas, the data is structured in different data sets known as aspects. An **aspect** consists of characteristics or dimensions and key figures. **Characteristics** classify the data by a dimension such as division, region, department, or company, whereas **key figures** are the data measured such as revenue, fixed costs, variable costs, number of employees, or quantities produced. Each aspect contains the data for a different business purpose. One aspect may be defined for logistics, while another is established for human resources. Data can be analyzed using report collections that are created individually for specific requirements. These reports are then accessed as needed. An example of a predefined EIS report in logistics is the Customer Analysis: Invoiced Sales report. You display this report and its related graphics for your review.

To examine the Customer Analysis: Invoiced Sales report:

1. Expand **Information Systems** on the SAP Easy Access menu, expand **Logistics,** expand **Sales and distribution,** expand **Customer,** and double-click **Sales** to display the Selection screen.

2. Type **1400*** in the first **Material** text box and **2000*** in the "to" **Material** text box; type **1000** in the **Sales Organization** text box; and then type **01.1998** in the first **Month** text box as the beginning date and **12.2000** in the "to" **Month** text box as the ending date. Notice here that the date is displayed as *month.year.* The display and entry format of the date is controlled as a user preference. Your instructor may show you how to change your preferred format, or you can check it out in SAP R/3 Help.

3. Type **usd** in the **Analysis Currency** text box to specify this as the currency that will be used. (See **Figure 11.36.**) All data is converted to this currency for the report.

4. Click the **Execute** button on the Application toolbar to complete the selection of this data and to display the Basic List with the data displayed by distribution channel. You want the data displayed by material.

5. Click the **Switch drilldown...** button Switch drilldown... to display that dialog box, click the **Material** option button, and then click the **Continue (Enter)** button .

6. Click **Invoiced Sales** in the report heading to select that column, and then click the **Sort in descending order** button to sort the data in the selected column. (See **Figure 11.37.**)

7. Click the **Graphics** button on the Application toolbar to display the Graphic: Choose Key Figure dialog box.

FIGURE 11.36
Customer Analysis:
Invoiced Sales:
Selection Screen

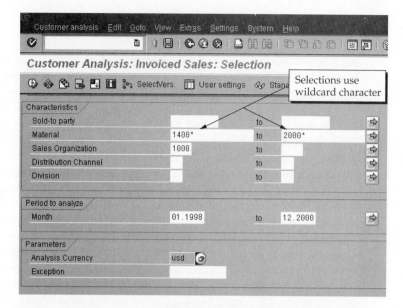

FIGURE 11.37
Customer Analysis:
Invoiced Sales:
Selection Screen

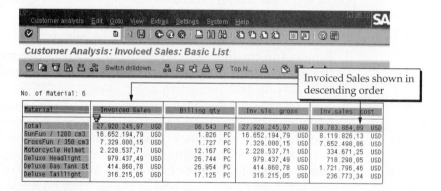

8. Click the **Invoiced Sales** check box and the **Billing quantity** check box to unselect these key figures.

9. Click the **Continue (Enter)** button ![checkmark] to display the Customer Analysis: Invoiced Sales graph in the SAP Business Graphics window. (See **Figure 11.38.**) Notice how the sort descending placed the largest values at the back of the 3D graphic so the smaller values are more visible.

10. Click the **Overview** button Overview on the Application toolbar to display a graphic with a Key figure comparison graph. (See **Figure 11.39.**)

11. Click the **Right** button Right on the Application toolbar to display a graph with the Material. (See **Figure 11.40.**)

12. Click **Motorcycle Helmet** in the Material list to select that material and display a graph for that material. (See **Figure 11.41.**)

Review the bar chart and compare the gross invoice sales to the invoice sales cost.

What are the gross invoice sales for Motorcycle Helmet? _____

FIGURE 11.38
Customer Analysis:
Invoiced Sales 3D
Graph of Key
Figures

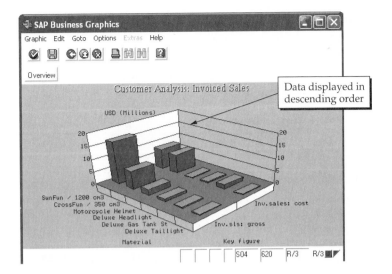

FIGURE 11.39
Customer Analysis:
Invoiced Sales
Comparison Graph
of Key Figures

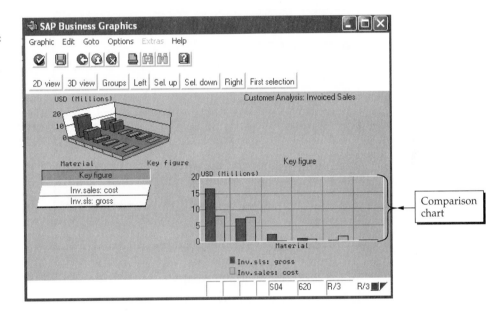

Now you are ready to return to the Basic List and then to the SAP Easy Access menu.

13. Click the **Exit** button 🔘 to close the graph. Click the **Exit** button 🔘 to return to Customer Analysis: Invoiced Sales: Basic List. Select **No** to saving data.

Click the **Exit** button 🔘 again to return to the main SAP Easy Access menu.

Logging Off from R/3

When you have completed using the R/3 System, you need to log off. The best practice is to log off from the R/3 System and not just to close your web browser. That way, you know that your session with the R/3 System was ended.

FIGURE 11.40
Customer Analysis:
Invoiced Sales
Comparison Graph
of Material

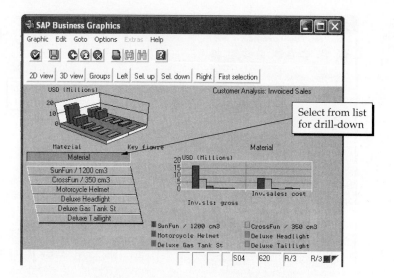

FIGURE 11.41
Customer Analysis:
Invoiced Sales
Detail Comparison
of Motorcycle
Helmet

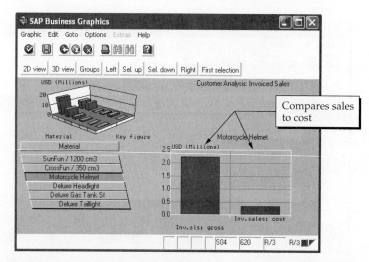

To log off from the R/3 System:

1. If necessary, return to the SAP Easy Access menu.

2. Click the **Log off** button 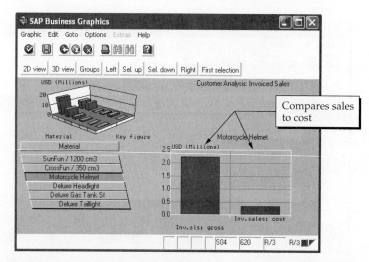 to display the Log Off dialog box; then click the **Yes** button to complete logging off from the R/3 System.

You have explored displaying summarized information from the R/3 System in several different forms that include R/3 EIS predefined reports.

Predefined reports were used to obtain summary information that was drawn from the R/3 database for a number of supporting transactions. This is only a small sample of the available reports in the SAP R/3 System. Many more reports are available or can be created for accessing information in the R/3 database.

Processing SAP R/3 Transactions

Part **3**

12

Customer Order to Cash Cycle Processes

Besides displaying or looking at data for individual transactions, you can enter the data that is created and stored when you enter or process a transaction. In the SAP R/3 system a transaction is a self-contained unit. Examples are tasks such as generating a list of customers, changing the address of a customer, booking a flight reservation for a customer, or executing a program. The transactions that you will be processing in the following activities include the creation of a customer master, a material master, and a vendor master. Also covered in these activities are sales order processing (creating, updating, and posting a sales order), delivery processing (including delivery, picking, and transferring), goods issued, and payment processing.

Master Data: Customer Master

A new customer contacted one of your salespeople. Your salesperson then conducted a telephone interview and collected all the relevant information and data. He then logged the customer's data into your **Master Data.**

In SAP all business transactions are posted to and managed in account records. The master record contains data that controls how business transactions are recorded and processed by the system. It also includes all the information about a customer that you need in order to conduct business with him or her.

Both the accounting (FI-AR) and the sales (SD) departments of your organization use customer master records. By storing a customer's master data, you enable it to be accessed throughout your organization and avoid the need to repeatedly enter the same information. You can also avoid inconsistencies in master data by maintaining it in one place in the R/3 database. If the address of one of your customers changes, for example, you only have to enter this change once, and your accounting and sales departments will always have up-to-date information. Specifications you make in master records are used for several things. They are used as default values when you post items to the account. For example, the terms of payment you specify in the master record are defaulted for document entry. The specifications are also used for processing business transactions, like account control data and the number of the G/L reconciliation accounts. For example, the date of the last dunning notice and the address are required for the automatic dunning process. When working with master records, you can prevent certain users from accessing an account by setting up authorization groups. When communicating with the customer, the specifications you set are also important, such as the address, telephone, and fax numbers. The specifications are also used in the sales department, order processing, shipping, and billing data.

To create a new Customer record:

1. Expand or double-click **Logistics** on the SAP Easy Access menu, expand **Sales and Distribution,** expand **Master Data,** expand **Business Partner,** expand **Customer,** and expand **Create.** See **Figure 12.1.** Then double-click **Complete** to start creating your own sold-to party.

Recall that you can launch an R/3 System transaction by carrying out the SAP Easy Access menu selection as shown in **Figure 12.1,** or you can enter the transaction code (**XD01** for the Complete selection) in the Command text box on the Standard toolbar. If this was a transaction that you executed frequently, you could also place a reference to this transaction in your Favorites in the SAP Easy Access menu. The SAP Easy Access standard menu selections are shown for this and the other transactions to help you become familiar with their location within the R/3 System.

2. The Customer Create: Initial Screen displays. The Account group that will be used for creating this customer is Sold-to party. Click the **Account group Search**

FIGURE 12.1
Application Tree to Create Customer

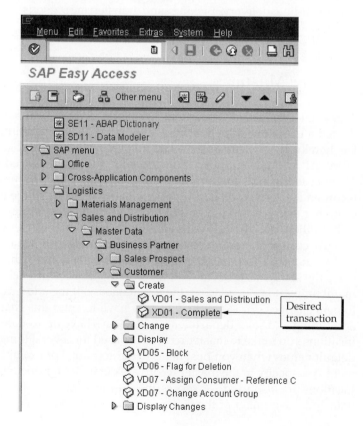

FIGURE 12.2
Customer Create:
Initial Screen

Customer Create: Initial Screen

Account group ☒ Sold-to party ▤
Customer ⊞ [ ] ← No Customer number

Company code 3000

Sales area
Sales Organization 3000
Distribution Channel 10
Division 00 ⊡

[All sales areas...] [Customer's sales areas...]

Reference
Customer ⊞ [ ]
Company code [ ]
Sales organization [ ]
Distribution channel [ ]
Reference division [ ]

✔ ⊞ ⊘ ⊗ ✖

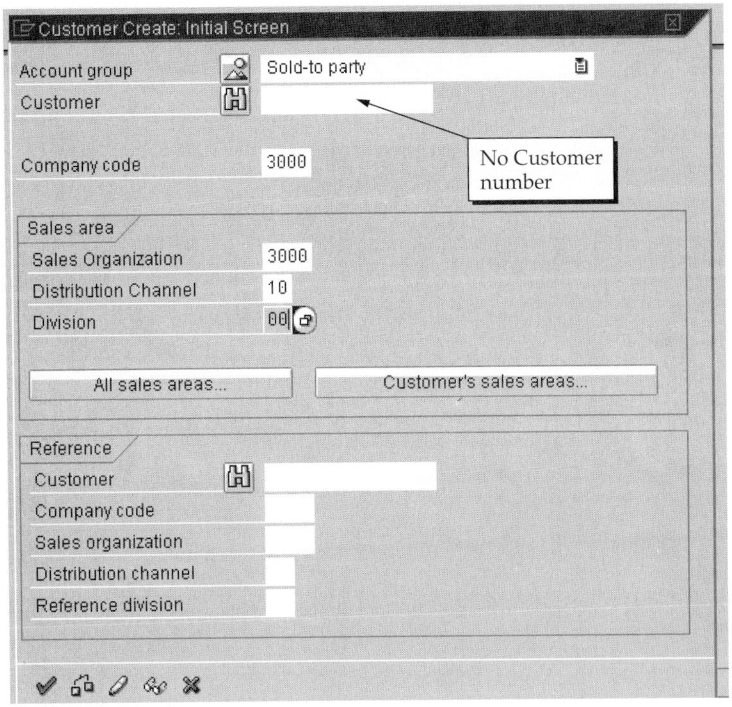

Help list button ▤, scroll the list to the Sold-to party, and then click **Sold-to party** to select it. Type **3000** in the **Company code** field. In the Sales area data section, three entries need to be made: type **3000** for the **Sales Organization,** type **10** as the **Distribution Channel,** and type **00** as the **Division. (See Figure 12.2.)** Click the **Continue (Enter)** button ✅, or press the **Enter** key. The Customer field, which is the number for the customer, remains blank because this number will be internally generated by the R/3 System since this is a new customer.

3. This will now bring you to the Create Customer: General Data screen. The next step is to enter the required information describing the customer. You can use any information you want here. On the **Address** tab, be sure to name your company (be creative!), and to add part of the name to the **Search term 1/2** box. This will help someone looking for your company who does not know the company code. He or she can enter part of the company name, and the search will find your company code. (See **Figure 12.3.**)

4. Completely fill out the **Address** tab and the **Contact persons** tab. Make sure you enter **English** as the language in the Communication section on the Address tab! If necessary, use the Tab scroll arrows to display the Contact persons tab. Type the first and last names of the contact person selected. (See **Figure 12.4.**)

5. If necessary, scroll the screen, and then click the **Details of partner selected** button 🔲 in the lower-left corner (**Figure 12.4**) to display the Create Customer: Contact Person Details screen. Type the following information: the **VIP**

FIGURE 12.3
Address Tab of
Create Customer
Screen

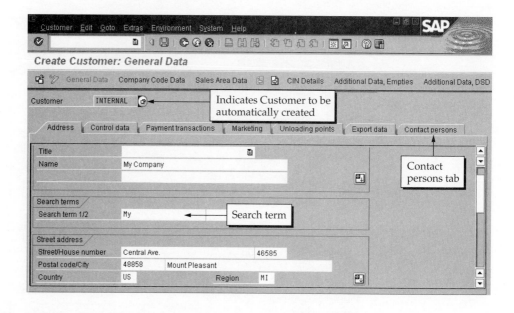

FIGURE 12.4
Contact Persons Tab
of Create Customer
Screen

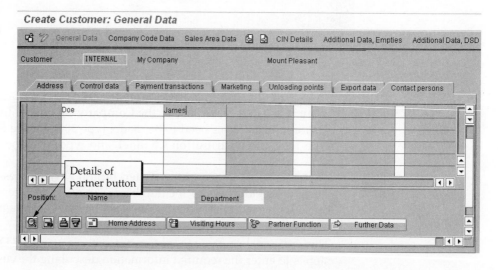

is **1,** the **Department** number is **0003,** the **Function** is **03,** and the **Power of att**
is **H.** Then press the **Enter** key. (See **Figure 12.5.**)

6. Click the **Visiting Hours** button in the Application toolbar (left side of
the screen). Choose a time for visiting hours for Monday morning and for
Wednesday afternoon. (See **Figure 12.6.**)

7. After entering the visiting hours, click the **Continue (Enter)** button to return to the Contact Person Details screen. Next, click the **Additional Data** button in the Application toolbar (right side of screen). This displays the Further
Data screen. Here you can enter some of the hobbies of your contact person.
Choose a few hobbies that you like. (See **Figure 12.7.**) When you are finished,

click the **Continue (Enter)** button .

FIGURE 12.5
Create Customer:
Contact Person
Details Screen

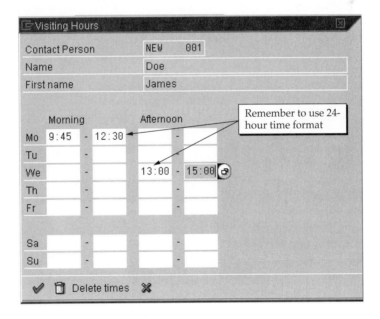

FIGURE 12.6
Visiting Hours

8. Click the **Back** button 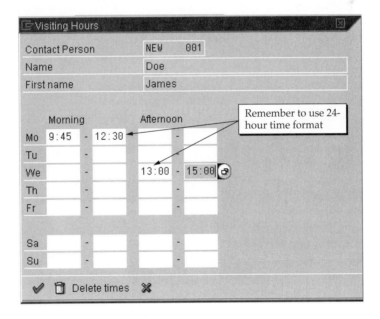 to return to the **Create Customer: General Data** screen. Click the **Sales Area Data** button on the Application toolbar. Type **A** in the **ABC class** text box. (See **Figure 12.8.**) Scroll to the Pricing/statistics section; then type **1** in the **Cust.price.proc** text box.

FIGURE 12.7
Further Data Screen

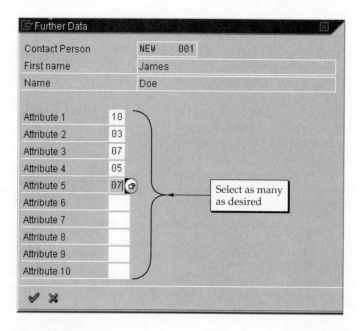

FIGURE 12.8
Change Customer: Sales Area Data

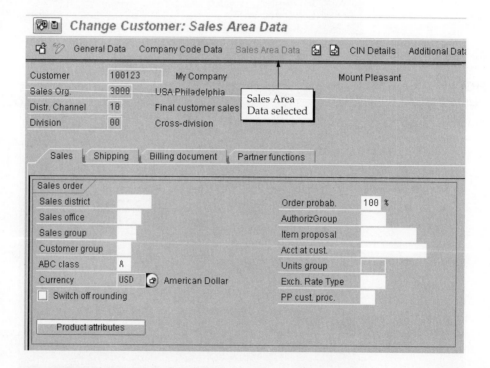

9. Click the **Shipping** tab. Type **01** in **Delivery Priority** to set the priority to high. Next, type **02** for the **Shipping conditions,** which specifies this as the standard shipping method. (See **Figure 12.9.**)

10. Click the **Billing document** tab. Scroll down to the Taxes section, and type **0** for **Taxes** in each row. (See **Figure 12.10.**) If necessary, scroll the list in the Taxes section in order to enter **0** for all the listed countries.

FIGURE 12.9
Shipping Tab

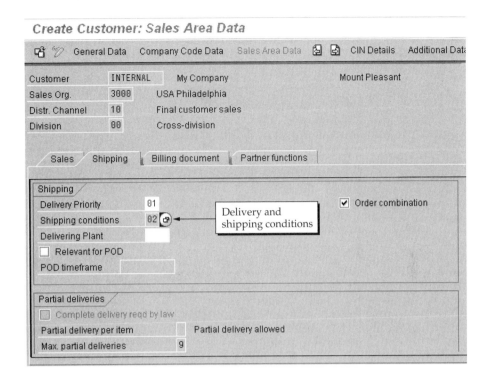

FIGURE 12.10
Billing Document
Tab

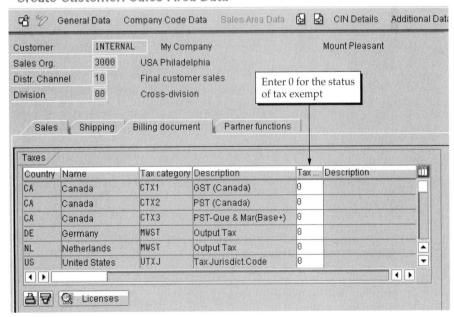

11. Click the **Company Code Data** button on the Application toolbar, and check for display of the **Account management** tab; if necessary, click that tab to display it. For the **Rec. Account,** type **140000,** which is the number for Trade Receivables—Domestic. (See **Figure 12.11.**)

FIGURE 12.11
Account
Management Tab

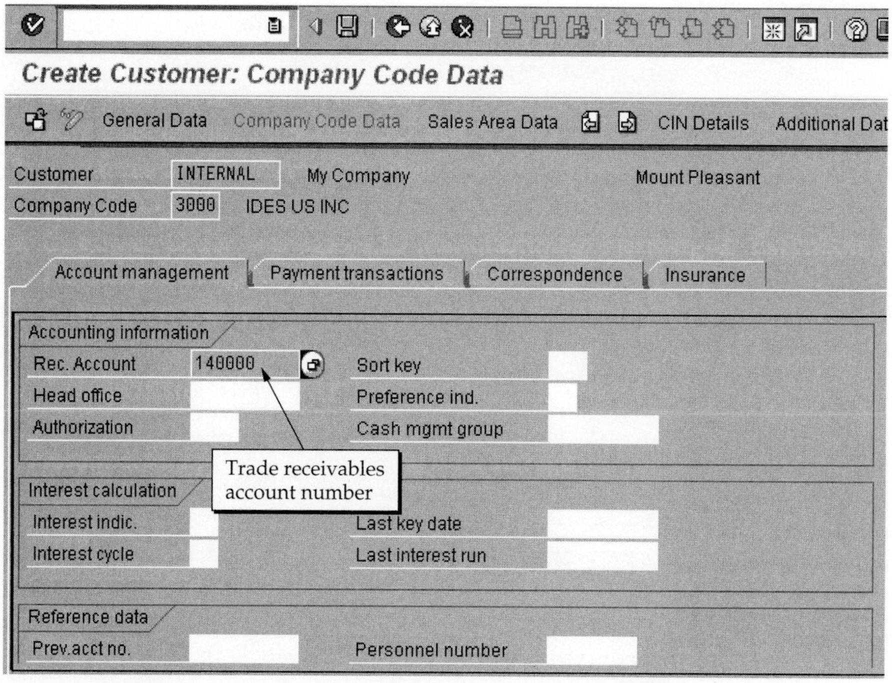

Create Customer: Company Code Data

General Data   Company Code Data   Sales Area Data   CIN Details   Additional Dat

| Customer | INTERNAL | My Company | Mount Pleasant |
| Company Code | 3000 | IDES US INC | |

Account management   Payment transactions   Correspondence   Insurance

Accounting information

Rec. Account	140000	Sort key	
Head office		Preference ind.	
Authorization		Cash mgmt group	

Trade receivables
account number

Interest calculation

| Interest indic. | | Last key date | |
| Interest cycle | | Last interest run | |

Reference data

| Prev. acct no. | | Personnel number | |

FIGURE 12.12
Customer Number
Displays in
Status Bar

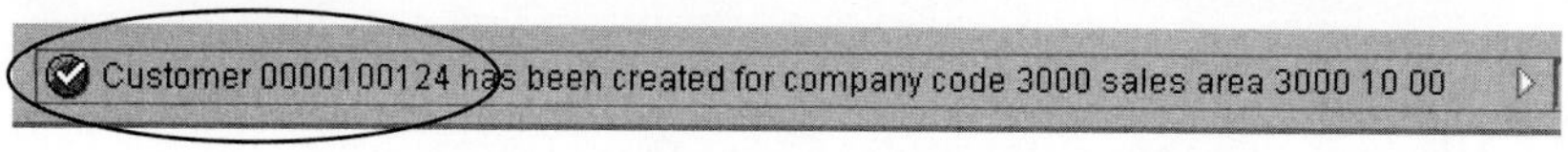

Customer 0000100124 has been created for company code 3000 sales area 3000 10 00

12. Click the **Payment transactions** tab and enter **0002** as the **Terms of payment.**

13. Finally, click the **Save** button on the Standard toolbar to finish creating a new customer (also known as a sold-to party). Your sold-to party is created, and the Customer number displays in the Status bar. (See **Figure 12.12.**)

14. Record the Customer number that you created.

1 Sold-to party: _____

(You will need this for future steps). You have now successfully created a sold-to party entity, also known as a customer.

Trouble? If when you click the **Save** button, the Create Customer: Initial Screen appears, simply drag it up and to the side so that you can obtain your Customer number (which is located in the Status bar at the bottom of your screen).

15. Click the **Exit** button to return to the SAP Easy Access menu.

Trouble? If you did not note your customer number, you can still find it after you close the Customer Create: Initial Screen. Double-click **Complete** on the SAP Easy Access menu, click the **Customer Search Help** button, type your search text in the **Search Term** text box, and then click the **Start Search (Enter)** button. This displays the Customer Account Number dialog box with the customer number, which was generated automatically by the R/3 System. See **Figure 12.12.** Click the **Close** button for the dialog box once you note the customer number.

Trouble?

If you made an error in entering any of your data, you can change that data. Double-click **Complete** on the SAP Easy Access menu, click the **Customer Search Help** button, type your search text in the **Search Term** text box, and click the **Start Search (Enter)** button to display the customer numbers. Then double-click the desired customer row to select it and return to the Customer Create: Initial Screen dialog box. Click the **Change** button to begin changing any desired data. When you are done, click the **Save** button on the Standard toolbar. Finally, use the **Exit** button to return to the SAP Easy Access menu.

Master Data: Material Record

A material master record is a data record containing all the basic information required to manage a material. This data is sorted according to various criteria. A material master record contains data of a descriptive nature (such as size, dimension, and weight) and data with a control function (such as material type and industry sector). In addition to this data, which can be directly maintained by the user, it also contains data that is automatically updated by the system (such as stock levels).

To create a material record:

1. Expand **Logistics;** then expand **Materials Management.** Expand **Material Master,** expand **Material,** and then expand **Create (Special).** (See **Figure 12.13.**)

2. Double-click **Finished Product** to select that transaction. This displays the Create Finished Product: Initial Screen. In the **Material** box, type the **B1000-##. (The ## is a two digit number that you obtain from your instructor and**

FIGURE 12.13
Create Material Menu Path

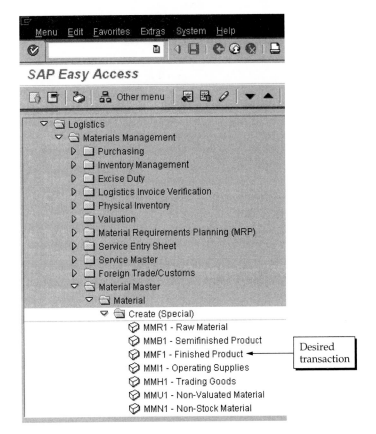

provides a unique identification for your material.) Click the **Industry Sector** box, and choose **Mechanical Engineering** from the drop-down menu. (See

Figure 12.14.) Then press the **Enter** key, or click the **Enter** button .

3. Select the views you want to be able to access. For this material, you are going to choose **Basic Data 1, Sales: Sales Org. Data 1** and **Data 2, Sales: General/Plant Data, MRP 1** and **2, Accounting 1,** and **Costing 1.** Once all these views are

selected, click the **Continue (Enter)** button . (See **Figure 12.15.**)

FIGURE 12.14
Create Finished Product: Initial Screen

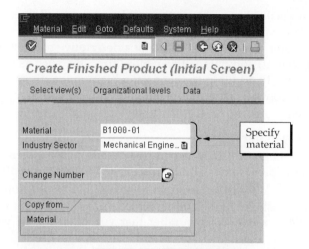

FIGURE 12.15
Select View(s) Screen

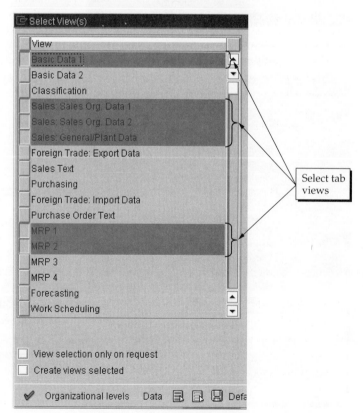

FIGURE 12.16
Organizational
Levels Screen

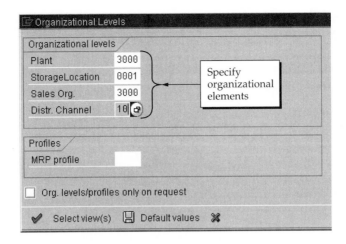

Trouble?

If the desired view does not appear in the Select view(s) dialog box, scroll the list so you can select the requested views.

4. The Organizational Levels dialog box displays. Type **3000** as the **Plant** number and **0001** as the **StorageLocation**. Type **3000** for the **Sales Org.** and **10** as the

   Distr. Channel. Click the **Continue (Enter)** button 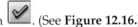. (See **Figure 12.16**.)

5. The default will display the Basic data 1 tab. You are now going to enter data that describes this material. You will see a check mark in all the fields that are required (known specifically in R/3 as **obligatory fields,** which must have a value entered before you can leave that screen tab). First is the **Material** text box, in which you enter the material's description. Type **Motorcycle** in this box. Next, click the **Base Unit of Measure** text box to select it, and open its Search Help. Scroll the list as needed to locate PC, which specifies pieces as the unit of measure. Double-click **PC** to choose it. Finally, you are going to display the possible entries list for the **Material Group.** Locate this text box and select **009** using Search Help. Enter values for both the **Net weight,** which is **7,** and the **Gross weight,** which is **9.** (See **Figure 12.17**.) Press the **Enter** key or click

   the **Enter** button .

6. The Sales: sales org. 1 tab should display. The only data that is necessary on this tab is the Tax Classification. Click the **Conditions** button, type **0** ("0" means tax exempt) in each of the spaces provided (there will probably be six). Be sure to scroll this list as needed and to type **0** for each entry in the Tax data section.

   Enter a **Scale quantity** of **1** and an **Amount** of **350.** Click the **Back** button .

   (See **Figure 12.18**.) Press the **Enter** key or click the **Enter** button . This will display the Sales: sales org. 2 tab. Select **Enter** again to skip this screen.

7. The Sales: general/plant tab should now display. Here you must key in the **Trans. grp** (transportation group) as **0001** and the **LoadingGrp** as **0002.** These are both required data entries you must specify before you can leave this tab

   screen. (See **Figure 12.19**.) Press the **Enter** key or click the **Enter** button .

FIGURE 12.17
Create Finished
Product, Basic Data
1 tab

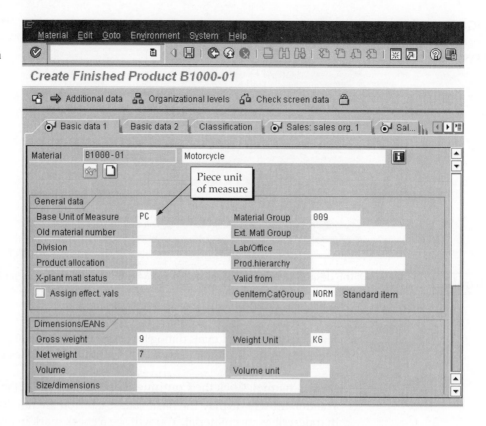

FIGURE 12.18
Create Finished
Product, Sales: Sales
Org. 1 tab

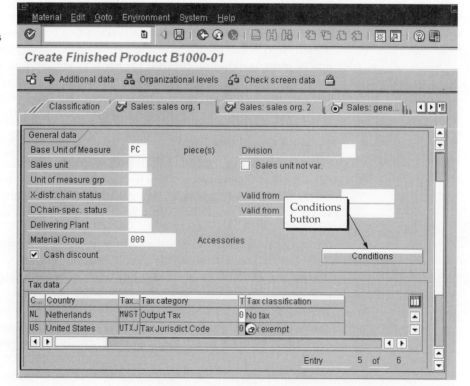

FIGURE 12.19
Create Finished
Product, Sales:
General/Plant tab

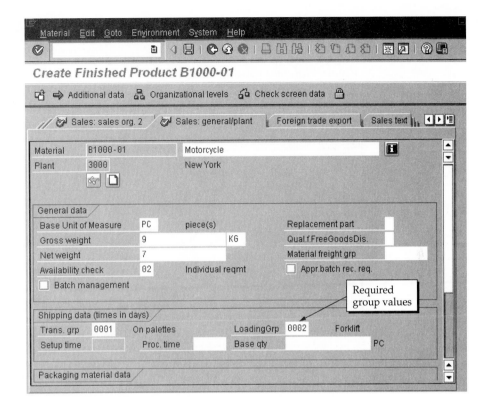

8. The **MRP 1** tab screen displays next. Here you must type the **MRP Type** as **PD,** the **MRP Controller** as **001,** and the **Lot size** as **EX.** (See **Figure 12.20.**) Press the **Enter** key or click the **Enter** button ![checkmark].

9. Next the MRP 2 tab screen displays. Type the **In-house production** as **5** days and the **SchedMargin key** (scheduled margin key) as **000.** Press **Enter** or click the **Enter** button ![checkmark].

10. Finally, the Accounting 1 tab screen displays. Here you will enter information about the price of your material. In the Current valuation section, in the **Valuation Class** field, specify **7920.** Locate the **Price Control** field, and type **S.** Then type **350.00** into the **Standard Price** field. (See **Figure 12.21.**) Press **Enter** or click the **Enter** button ![checkmark] to proceed to the Costing 1 screen. No additional data is entered in this screen. You are ready to save this data, so click the **Save** button ![save].

11. You have now created a **Material Master record.** Click the **Save** button ![save] again to save all your data. A message will appear at the bottom of your screen in the Status bar that this material has been created. Write down the Material number for future use.

 Material number: _____

FIGURE 12.20
Create Finished
Product, MRP 1 tab

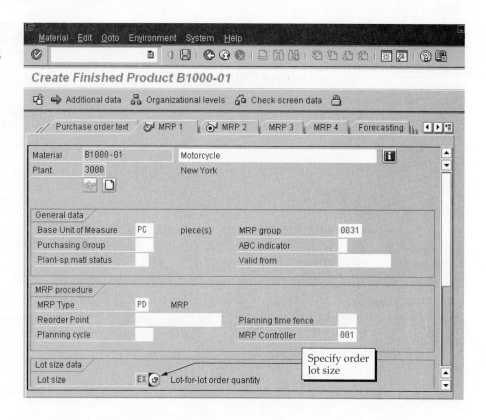

FIGURE 12.21
Create Finished
Product, Accounting
1 tab

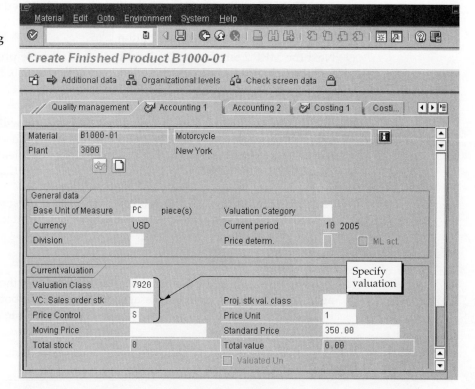

Trouble?

If you made a mistake in entering any of your data, you must change it. You can use Change so that you can update an existing Material; it simply must be changed. From **Material** in the SAP Easy Access menu, select **Change,** select **Immediately,** and then enter the Material, which is its number. Press **Enter** or click the **Enter** button. You can now select the desired views (tabs) and make changes to your initial data entries.

12. Click the **Exit** button to return to the SAP Easy Access screen.

Master Data: Vendor Record

A vendor is a business partner from whom materials or services can be procured. The **Vendor master record** is a data record containing all the information necessary for any contact with a certain vendor, in particular for carrying out business transactions. This information includes, for example, address data and bank data.

To create a Vendor record:

1. From the SAP Easy Access screen, open the **Logistics** folder. Click **Materials Management,** click **Purchasing,** click **Master Data,** click the **Vendor** folder, and click **Central.** (See **Figure 12.22.**)

2. Double-click **Create** to display the Create Vendor: Initial Screen. Four fields need to be filled out on this screen. The first is the **Vendor** name. Type **123##,** (where ## is the number you used for your material master). Next you are going to type the **Company Code,** which is **3000.** Type **3000** for the **Purch. organization.** In the **Account group** field, use Search Help to select **LIEF.** (See **Figure 12.23.**) Press the **Enter** key or click the **Enter** button .

3. For the **Name,** type **Purchasing Vendor – ##.** (Again the ## is the same two-digit number you obtained from your instructor.) You will also need to enter a **Search term 1/2.** This is used when you are conducting a search and you want to be able

FIGURE 12.22
**Create Vendor
Menu Path**

```
▽ 🗎 Materials Management
   ▽ 🗎 Purchasing
      ▷ 📁 Purchase Order
      ▷ 📁 Purchase Requisition
      ▷ 📁 Outline Agreement
      ▷ 📁 RFQ/Quotation
      ▽ 🗎 Master Data
         ▷ 📁 Info Record
         ▷ 📁 Source List
         ▷ 📁 Quota Arrangement
         ▷ 📁 Approved Manufacturer Parts
         ▽ 🗎 Vendor
            ▷ 📁 Purchasing
            ▽ 🗎 Central
               📦 XK01 - Create ◀————  [ Desired transaction ]
               📦 XK02 - Change
               📦 XK03 - Display
               📦 XK04 - Changes
               📦 XK05 - Block
               📦 XK06 - Flag for Deletion
               📦 XK07 - Account Group Change
            ▷ 📁 List Displays
```

FIGURE 12.23
Create Vendor:
Initial Screen

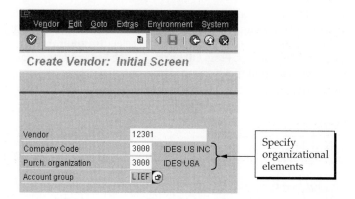

FIGURE 12.24
Create Vendor:
Address Screen

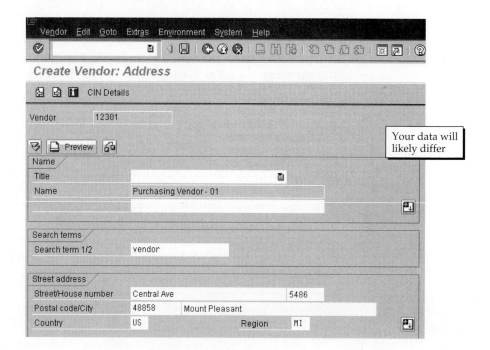

to find your vendor. Use any single word that you would easily remember. Fill in the rest of the address data on your own. Be creative! (See **Figure 12.24.**) When you are finished filling in the information, press the **Enter** key or click the

Enter button 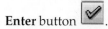.

4. After you press the **Enter** key, the Control screen displays. Skip this and go to the next screen by pressing the **Enter** key again. The next screen is the Create Vendor: Payment transactions screen—you also skip this one. Press the **Enter** key again to advance to the Create Vendor: Accounting information Accounting screen.

5. In the Accounting information section, for the **Rec. Account** (reconciliation account), type **160000.** In the **Cash mgmnt group** field, type **A1.** (See **Figure 12.25.**)

Press the **Enter** key or click the **Enter** button .

FIGURE 12.25
Create Vendor:
Accounting
Information
Accounting Screen

Create Vendor: Accounting information Accounting

CIN Details

Vendor	12301	Purchasing Vendor - 01	Mount Pleasant
Company Code	3000	IDES US INC

General Ledger
account number

Accounting information

Rec. Account	160000	Sort key
Head office		Subsidy indic.
Authorization		Cash mgmnt group	A1	Domestic
		Release group
Minority indic.		Certificatn date

FIGURE 12.26
Create Vendor:
Payment
Transactions
Accounting Screen

Create Vendor: Payment transactions Accounting

CIN Details

Vendor	12301	Purchasing Vendor - 01	Mount Pleasant
Company Code	3000	IDES US INC

Payment data

Payment terms	ZB00	Tolerance group
		Chk double inv.
Chk cashng time		

Automatic payment transactions

Payment methods	CT	Payment block		Free for payment
Alternat.payee		House bank	3000
Individual pmnt		Grouping key
B/exch.limit		USD
Pmt adv. by EDI		

Specify bank
for payment

6. The Create Vendor: Payment transactions Accounting screen displays. Here you will enter information about the terms of payment. In the Payment data section, for **Payment terms,** type **ZB00.** In the Automatic payment transactions section, type **CT** for the **Payment methods** and type **3000** for the **House bank.** A **house bank** is your company's bank where you have an account with them. (See **Figure 12.26.**) Press the **Enter** key or click the **Enter** button .

7. The next screen, which is the Create Vendor: Correspondence Accounting screen, is skipped by pressing the **Enter** key. This displays the Create Vendor: Purchasing data screen. In the Conditions section type **USD** as the **Order currency,** and again type **ZB00** as the **Terms of payment.** Finally, in the **Incoterms** fields, type **FOB** in the first (left) field and **Philadelphia** in the second (right) field. (See **Figure 12.27.**) Press the **Enter** key or click the **Enter** button .

8. The next screen is the Create Vendor: Partner function screen. Press the **Enter** key to skip it and to display the Last data screen reached dialog box. Click the **Yes** button to save the data. The Create Vendor: Initial Screen displays again with a message in the Status bar indicating that the vendor has been created in the system. (See **Figure 12.28.**)

FIGURE 12.27
Purchasing Data
Screen

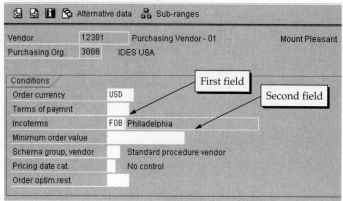

FIGURE 12.28
Vendor Number in
Status Bar

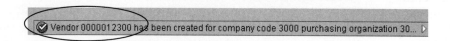

9. Record the Vendor number you created.

 Vendor number:_____

10. Click the **Exit** button ⬆ to return to the SAP Easy Access screen.

Sales Order Processing

The majority of your customers order their products without an inquiry or a quotation. The sales process normally begins when a customer calls to place a **sales order.** When recording the order, the customer service representative enters minimal information, such as order type, customer ID, and quantity. The R/3 System then calculates and completes the remaining information.

After entering the order, the customer service representative must answer questions relating to the order—both immediately after taking the order and anytime the customer calls with questions or updates. You are now going to create a sales order for an existing material in stock and a known vendor. Both of the characteristics are important considerations for the sales order.

To create a sales order:

1. From the SAP Easy Access menu, click **Logistics** to expand this menu, click **Sales and Distribution,** click **Sales,** and then click **Order** to open that folder. (See **Figure 12.29.**)
2. Double-click **Create.** This displays the Create Sales Order: Initial Screen. Now type **OR** as the **Order Type,** which is a standard order. In the Organizational data section, type **3000** for the **Sales Organization, 10** for the **Distribution Channel,** and **00** for the **Division.** (See **Figure 12.30.**) Press the **Enter** key or

click the **Enter** button ✓.
3. You should now be at the Create Standard Order: Overview screen. Click the **Sales** tab. Here you will enter data about your order. Enter your Customer

FIGURE 12.29
Create Sales Order
Menu Path

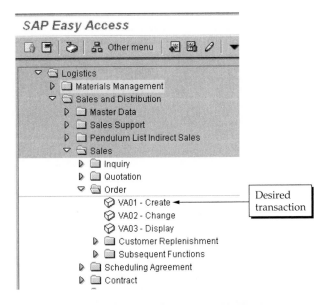

FIGURE 12.30
Create Sales Order:
Initial Screen

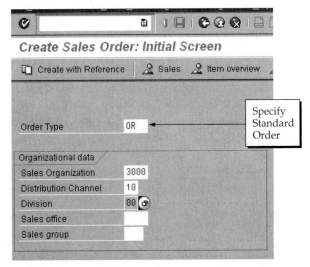

number, which you created in the Master Data: Customer Master transaction activity, in the **Sold to Party** field. Type **PO 560** for the **PO Number.** The **Purchase Order Date** is going to be Today's Date, and the **Req. delivery date** will be three days from today's date. Enter **ZB00** as the **Payment terms,** and **FOB Philadelphia** as the **Incoterms.** Incoterms is two fields, so one value goes in each field. The **Material** you will be using is **M-11,** with a **quantity** of **10.** After

typing this information, press the **Enter** key or click the **Enter** button ![enter button]. (See **Figure 12.31.**)

4. Click the **Save** button ![save button] to complete the order, and wait for this process to finish. The Standard Order number appears in the Status bar. (See **Figure 12.32.**) Record this number.

Standard Order number: _____

FIGURE 12.31
Create Standard
Order: Overview

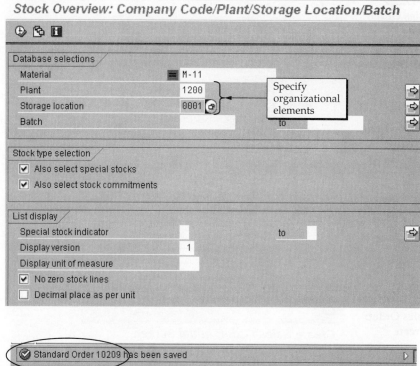

FIGURE 12.32
Standard Order
Number in Status
Bar

Trouble?

One or more information dialog boxes may pop up, telling you that the sales order or billing information has been re-determined. These are just information screens. Click the **Enter** button on these screens to skip them.

Trouble?

If when you save your sales order an information screen pops up, telling you that the document is incomplete and giving you a choice to save anyway or to edit, select edit. It will then tell you what is missing in the document. Double-click on the first item, and it will take you to where you need to edit the document. Once you have completed that screen, click on the green back-arrow to see if you have any more incomplete fields. Once the document is complete, it will return you to the Sales Order screen and say that the document is complete. Save the document again to get your sales order number.

5. Click the **Exit** button ![icon] to return to the SAP Easy Access screen. If you are asked if you want to save your data, click the **No** button, because you have already created and saved your standard order.

Stock Overview and Sales Order Update

After you created the sales order, the customer called back and wanted to add one more to the quantity ordered. You now have to **change the sales order.** But before you change the sales order, you need to make sure that there is enough of the **material in stock.**

FIGURE 12.33
Stock Overview
Menu Path

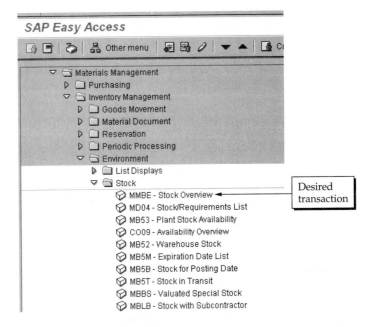

FIGURE 12.34
Stock Overview
Screen

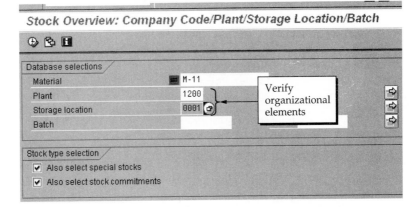

To create a stock overview:

1. On the SAP Easy Access menu, click **Logistics** and click **Materials Management.** Click **Inventory Management,** click **Environment,** and click **Stock.** (See **Figure 12.33.**)

2. Double-click **Stock Overview.** This displays the Stock Overview: Company Code/Plant/Storage Location/Batch screen. In the Database selections section, type your **Material** number (**M-11**) into the material field. Type **1200** for the **Plant,** and **0001** for the **Storage location.** (See **Figure 12.34.**) Click the **Execute** button ![execute button].

3. The **Stock Overview** screen for **Material M-11** displays. Look for the available amount of Unrestricted use stock. Is there enough to increase your customer's order by one and still have a good amount left in stock? If yes, then you can change the sales order. If the answer is no, then you will have to call your customer and say that at this time you are unable to process that amount of this particular material. (See **Figure 12.35.**)

FIGURE 12.35
Stock Overview
Results

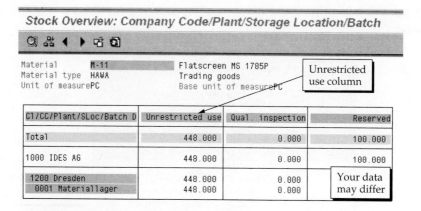

FIGURE 12.36
Change Sales Order
Menu Path

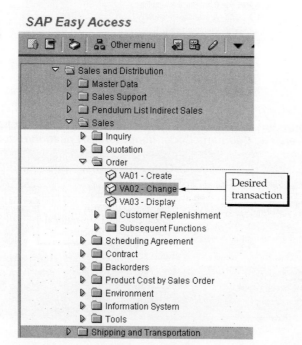

4. Click the **Exit** button to return to the SAP Easy Access screen.

You are now ready to change the sales order to increase the Quantity of Material M-11 by one for the increased order amount.

To update a sales order:

1. From the SAP Easy Access menu, click **Logistics,** and then click **Sales and Distribution.** Click **Sales** and click **Order.** (See **Figure 12.36.**)

2. Double-click **Change.** This displays the Change Sales Order: Initial Screen. If necessary, type your Sales Order number in the **Order** field. The R/3 System "remembers" this entry from your prior uses, so it may automatically appear for your use; in that case, just continue. (See **Figure 12.37.**) Press the **Enter** key.

3. An information screen may be displayed saying to "Consider the subsequent documents." Just press the **Enter** key to close the screen, and display the Change Standard Order #####: Overview screen.

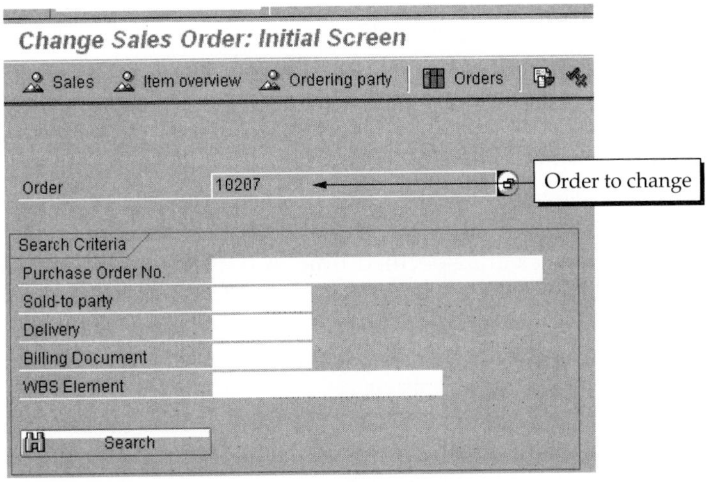

FIGURE 12.37
Change Sales Order: Initial Screen

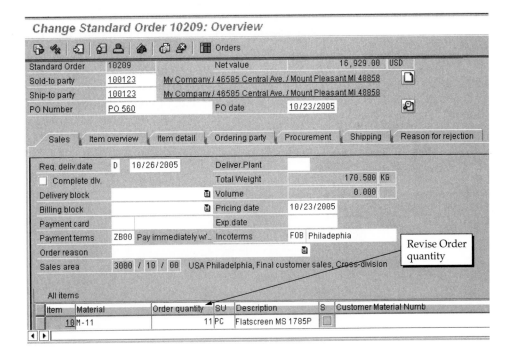

FIGURE 12.38
Change Standard Order ####: Overview Screen

4. Your customer wants the quantity ordered to be increased by one. So, add one to the **Order quantity,** and press the **Enter** key. (See **Figure 12.38.**) Click the **Save** button 💾 to complete the changes.

A message displays in the Status bar confirming that your Standard Order has been saved (refer to **Figure 12.32**), and you return to the Change Sales Order: Initial Screen.

5. Click the **Exit** button 🔙 to return to the SAP Easy Access screen. If you are asked if you want to save your data, click the **No** button.

The Delivery Process

Delivery within the R/3 System is considered as the process for receiving, sending, or transferring goods. The delivery can be either an inbound or an outbound delivery. You will be creating a delivery request, which is a request that includes all data relevant for a particular delivery. **Transfer orders** are instructions to move materials from a source storage bin to a destination storage bin within a warehouse complex at a specified time. A transfer order consists of items that contain the quantity of the material to be moved and specifies the source and destination storage bins. A transfer order can be created based on a customer delivery, a transfer requirement, or a posting change notice. Source and destination storage bins can be in different warehouses.

Now that you have updated the sales order, you are going to start the delivery process. First, you will specify where and when you want the order to be shipped.

To create a delivery request:

1. From the SAP Easy Access menu, click **Logistics;** then click **Sales and Distribution.** Click **Shipping and Transportation** and click **Outbound Delivery.** Next click **Create** and choose **Single Document.** (See **Figure 12.39.**)

2. Double-click **With Reference to Sales Order.** This displays the Create Outbound Delivery with Order Reference screen. Type **3000** for the **Shipping point.** In the Sales order data section, type the date you entered for the Req. deliv. date (three days from the date of your sales order) for the **Selection date** and your **Order** from the previous activity, if necessary, because this may again automatically display. (See **Figure 12.40.**) Press the **Enter** key or click the **Enter** button .

FIGURE 12.39
Delivery Menu Path

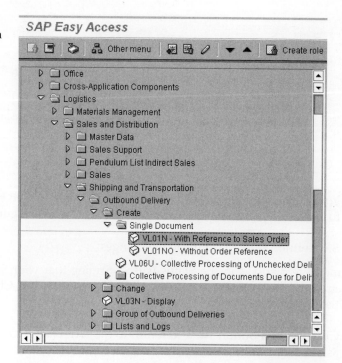

FIGURE 12.40
Create Outbound
Delivery with Order
Reference Screen

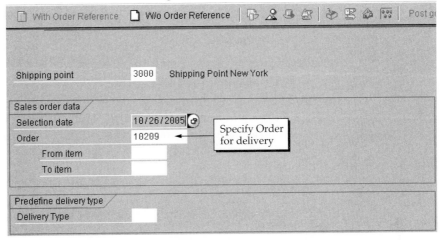

FIGURE 12.41
Delivery Create:
Overview Screen

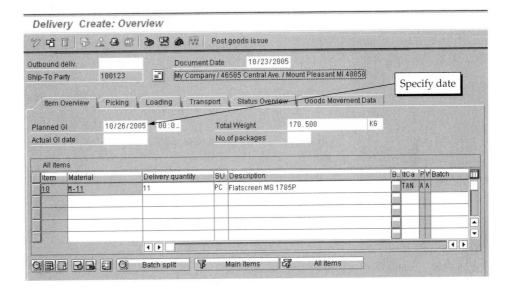

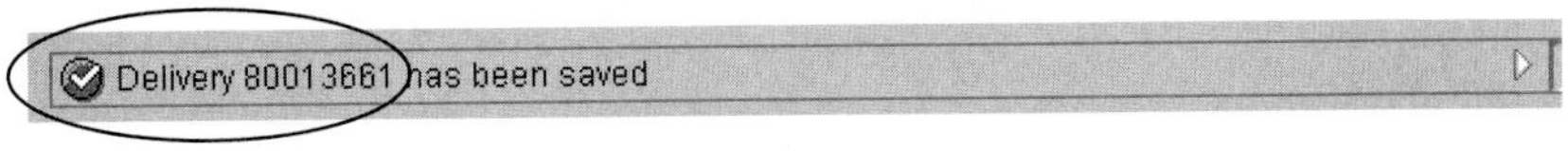

FIGURE 12.42
Delivery Number
Appears in Status
Bar

3. The Delivery Create: Overview screen displays. You may receive a note at the bottom of your screen with a message saying "Check the notes in the log." Do not worry about this. (See **Figure 12.41.**)

4. Click the **Save** button ![save icon], and record your Delivery number, which is automatically generated by the R/3 System. (See **Figure 12.42.**) Your number will likely be different.

Delivery number: _____

5. Click the **Exit** button 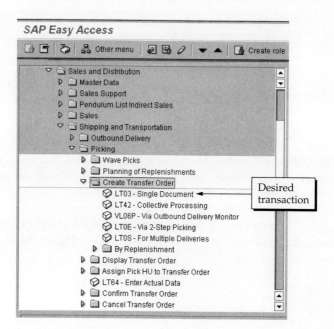 to return to the SAP Easy Access screen.

The Picking Process

The next step in the delivery process is the **picking process.** This is the process of issuing and grouping certain partial quantities (materials) from the warehouse on the basis of goods requirements from the Sales or the Production department. Picking can take place using transfer orders or picking lists. Picking from fixed storage bins and random picking are different actions and need to be distinguished.

To carry out the picking process:

1. Now you are going to complete the picking process. The SAP Easy Access menu should remain displayed. If it is not, follow the same menu path from the Delivery Process to reach **Shipping and Transportation** as the desired menu. After this folder is selected, click **Picking** and click **Create Transfer Order.** (See **Figure 12.43.**)

2. Double-click **Single Document.** This displays the Create Transfer Order for Delivery: Initial Screen. Type **300** for the **Warehouse Number,** and **3000** for the **Plant.** Your Delivery number should appear by default in the **Delivery** text box, but if it does not, enter the Delivery number that you received from the delivery

   process. (See **Figure 12.44.**) Press the **Enter** key or click the **Enter** button .

3. The Create TO for Delivery: Overview Deliveries screen displays. This is the transfer order for the delivery. (See **Figure 12.45.**)

4. Click the **Save** button . You will now get a Transfer Order number. (See **Figure 12.46.**) Your number will likely be different from the one shown next.

FIGURE 12.43
Picking Menu path

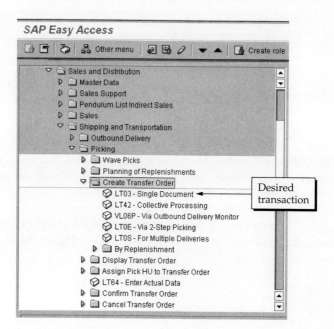

FIGURE 12.44
Create Transfer
Order for Delivery:
Initial Screen

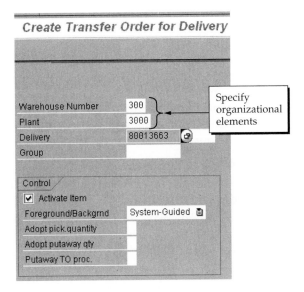

FIGURE 12.45
Create TO for
Delivery: Overview
Deliveries Screen

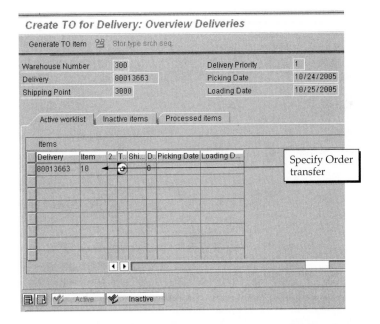

FIGURE 12.46
Transfer Order
Number Appears
in Status Bar

Transfer order 0000000443 created

5. Record the Transfer Order number.

Transfer Order number _____

6. Click the **Exit** button to return to the SAP Easy Access screen.

Document Flow

Your customer has now called back with an inquiry about the sales order. Inquiries often require tracking the sales order. This means that you want to see the document flow for that customer. A **document flow** is a representation in the system of the sequence of documents for a particular business transaction. A document flow could, for example, consist of a quotation, a sales order, a delivery, and an invoice. So, you are going to find out how that order is moving.

To view a document flow:

1. From the SAP Easy Access menu, click **Logistics,** click **Sales and Distribution,** select the **Sales** folder, and click **Order.** (See **Figure 12.47.**)
2. Double-click **Display.** This displays the Display Sales Order: Initial Screen. Your Order number should display there by default, but if not, type the number you received in the Sales Order Processing activity. (See **Figure 12.48.**) Press the **Enter** key.

FIGURE 12.47
Display Order
Menu Path

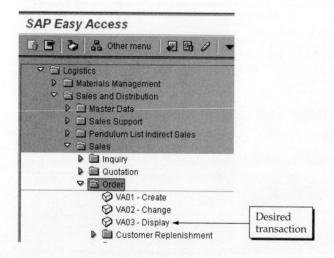

FIGURE 12.48
Display Sales
Order: Initial
Screen

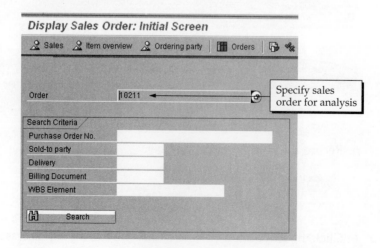

FIGURE 12.49
Display Document
Flow Menu Path

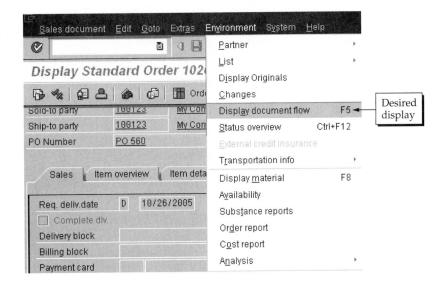

FIGURE 12.50
Document Flow
Screen

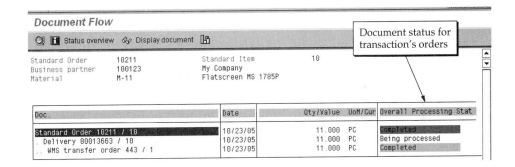

3. Click **Environment** on the Main menu; then click **Display document flow.** (See **Figure 12.49.**)

4. The Document Flow screen displays. Here you can see all the documents you have created and their current status. (See **Figure 12.50.**) Remember that yours may not look exactly the same as this one, and the data will likely be different.

5. Click the **Exit** button ![exit] to return to the sales order. Click the **Exit** button ![exit] again to return to the SAP Easy Access screen.

Goods Issue Document

The next step is to post a goods issue document. A **goods issue document** is a statement verifying goods movement and containing information for follow-up tasks. A corresponding material document is created for the outflow of material with the goods issue document in the delivery. The material document contains one or more items and can be printed as a goods receipt/issue slip for the actual physical movement of goods.

FIGURE 12.51
Post Goods Issue
Menu Path

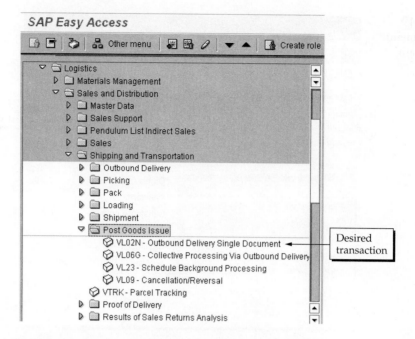

FIGURE 12.52
Change Outbound
Delivery Screen

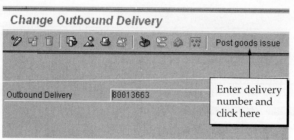

To post a goods issue:

1. From the SAP Easy Access menu, click **Logistics,** click **Sales and Distribution,** and click **Shipping and Transportation.** Click **Post Goods Issue.** (See **Figure 12.51.**)

2. Double-click **Outbound Delivery Single Document.** This displays the Change Outbound Delivery screen. Type your **Delivery number** created in the delivery process activity, if it does not appear automatically for you. Click the **Post goods issue** button ⬛ **Post goods issue** . (See **Figure 12.52.**)

3. A confirmation message will display at the bottom of your screen, saying that your delivery has been saved. (See **Figure 12.53.**)

4. Click the **Exit** button 🔘 to return to the SAP Easy Access screen.

Invoicing

The payment creates a pair of documents with the relevant invoice account assignment; the first line has status "Invoice" and the second has status "Payment" in the display. When the invoice has been cleared in full, it is converted to "Payment" status (all document lines are then flagged as "paid").

FIGURE 12.53
Confirmation
Message

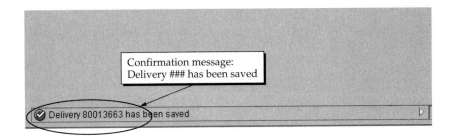

FIGURE 12.54
Billing Menu Path

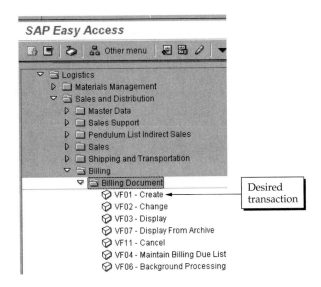

To invoice the customer:

1. The next step is to invoice the customer. From the SAP Easy Access menu, click **Logistics,** click **Sales and Distribution,** click **Billing,** and click **Billing Document.** (See **Figure 12.54.**)

2. Double-click **Create.** This displays the Create Billing Document screen. By default, the delivery number that you saved in the previous step should be entered in the **Document** field. If it is not, type the reference number in this field. (See **Figure 12.55.**)

3. Click the **Execute** button to go to the Invoice (F2) Create: Overview of Billing Items screen. Click the **Save** button . This will create a billing document, return you to the Create Billing Document screen, and display a number at the bottom of the screen in the Status bar. (See **Figure 12.56.**)

4. Record your document number from the Status bar here for future use.

Document number: _____

5. Click the **Exit** button to return to the SAP Easy Access screen.

FIGURE 12.55
**Create Billing
Document Screen**

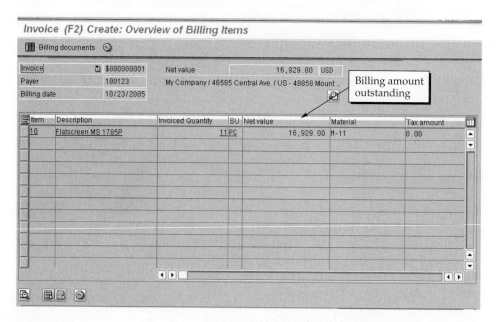

FIGURE 12.56
**Overview of Billing
Items Screen**

Incoming Payments

You need incoming payment flows if you want to post incoming payments from income (e.g., interest), repayments, or refunds of overpaid taxes via a receivables account. You first post a flow, which creates a receivable (account determination: receivable to income or receivable to position). When you actually receive the incoming payment, you then post an incoming payment flow, which clears this receivable again (account determination: bank clearing to receivable). Receivables flows are usually posted via the automatic posting function. At the same time, the system generates the incoming payments flows, which you then post via the incoming payments function. The incoming payments field manages whether and how the first receivables flow automatically generates a second flow during posting.

To process an incoming payment:

1. You have just received a payment of $28,083.44 from the customer. You now need to type the received payment into the system. From the SAP Easy Access menu, click **Accounting**, click **Financial Accounting**, click **Accounts Receivable,** and click **Document entry.** (See **Figure 12.57.**)

2. Double-click **Incoming payment.** This displays the Post Incoming Payments: Header Data screen. Type today's date for the **Document Date.** In the Bank

FIGURE 12.57
Incoming Payments
Menu Path

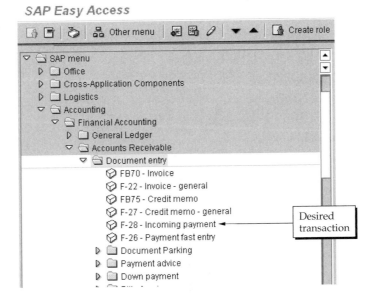

FIGURE 12.58
Posting Incoming
Payments Screen

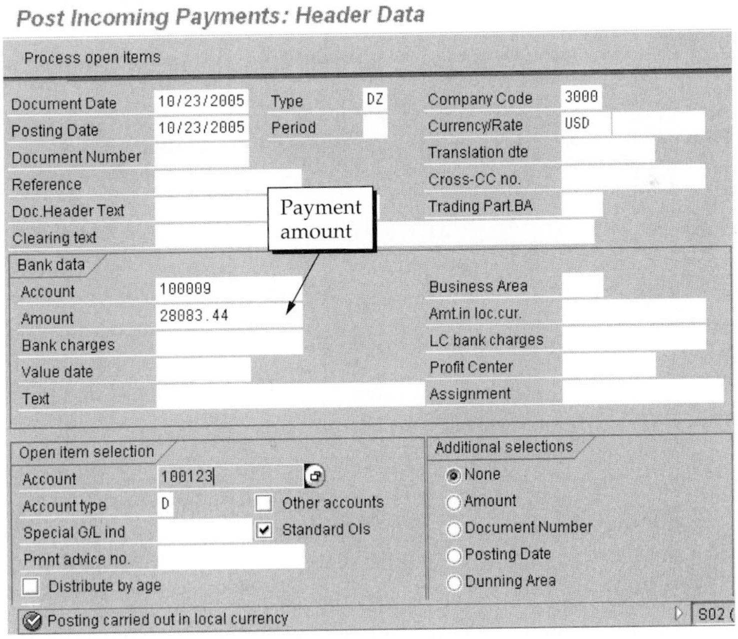

data section, type **28,083.44** for the **Amount,** and type **100009** for the **Account.** Under the Open item selection section, type the customer number for the **Account.** This is the number obtained previously in the Master Data: Customer Number processing activity. (See **Figure 12.58.**)

3. Click the **Process open items** button on the Menu bar. This displays the Post Incoming Payments: Process open items screen. Check to see that the **Not assigned** field says **0.00.** If not, look at the assigned amount and record it here: _____. Then click the **back arrow** twice. Reenter the above information, except put the assigned amount in the **Amount** field. Click the

Process open items button again. Finally, click the **Save** button 🖫 to post the payment. (See **Figure 12.59.**)

FIGURE 12.59
Process Open Items Screen

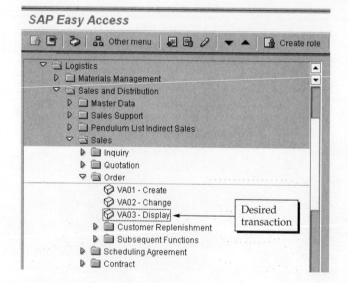

FIGURE 12.60
Display Document Flow Menu Path

4. Once the payment has been posted, the system will return to the Post Incoming Payments: Header Data screen. A Document number for the posting appears in the Status bar at the bottom of the screen as a confirmation for this transaction.

 Document number: _____

5. Click the **Exit** 🔙 button to return to the SAP Easy Access screen.
6. You want to display the document flow a second time, to ensure that all the business processes have been completed. Click **Logistics,** click **Sales and Distribution,** click **Sales,** and click **Order.** (See **Figure 12.60.**)

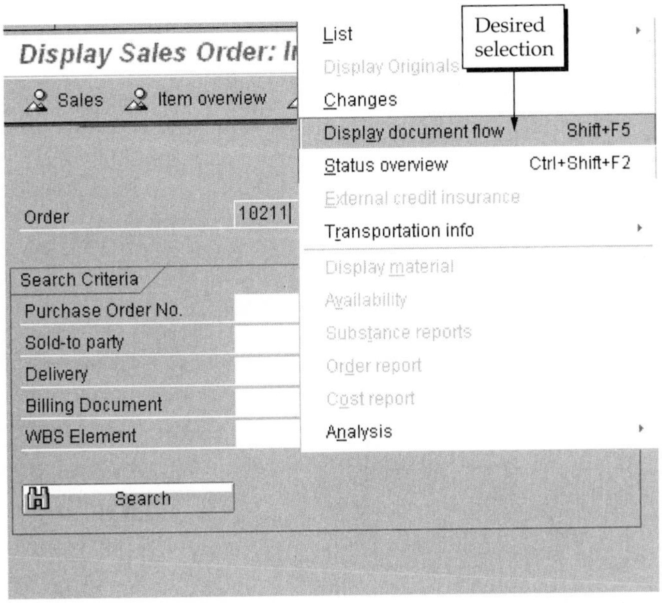

FIGURE 12.61
Display Document Flow

FIGURE 12.62
Document Flow Screen

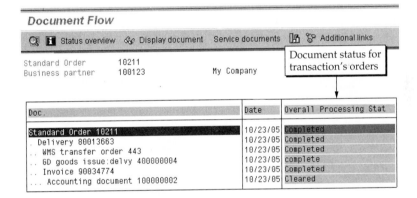

7. Double-click **Display.** This displays the Display Sales Order: Initial Screen. You will need your sales order number. Type your sales order number into the **Order** field. On the Application menu at the top of the screen, click **Environment,** and click **Display document flow.** (See **Figure 12.61.**)

8. This displays the Document Flow screen. Here you can see the documents you entered for the initial order, the delivery, the transfer, goods delivery, invoicing, and payments received. (See **Figure 12.62.**)

9. Click the **Exit** button 🔼 to return to the Display Sales Order: Initial Screen.

Click the **Exit** button 🔼 again to return to the SAP Easy Access screen.

10. Click the **Exit** button 🔼 once more to log off from the SAP R/3 system.

Summary

The SAP R/3 Enterprise system is software that encompasses most of the common business applications that organizations use to manage their daily activities. These business processes constitute the supply chain management activities found in many business organizations. The R/3 System uses a three-tier client/server architecture to implement processing for the presentation, application, and database components of this architecture. The SAP Web Application Server (SAP Web AS) is the middleware that guarantees all the SAP application modules are integrated and platform-independent across the entire complement of SAP products. SAP Web AS includes the ABAP programming language, a tool to build specialized user reports and transactions not provided directly by R/3 System business processes that are furnished by SAP AG.

Although the R/3 System has some unique characteristics, the SAPGUI provides a user interface that is similar to other Microsoft Windows applications. This permits users to enter data and to display information using the familiar environment of a Windows application. Because the R/3 System encompasses so many different business transactions, each end user typically learns to use the display screens for just a limited number of the R/3 transactions. End-user training familiarizes these users with the menu paths and data entry necessary to navigate the R/3 System and to process the transactions that are the responsibility of that end user. Possible values or matchcodes assist end users in making their selections when processing particular transactions within the R/3 System.

The R/3 System is Web-enabled through the use of an Internet Transaction Server. This allows a web browser to function as the client front-end for the R/3 System. The future of the R/3 System is for the expanded use of a web browser as the end user's client. This capability is supported by the SAP Web AS.

Implementation is a key aspect of the R/3 System. This involves the actual installation and configuration of the R/3 System to meet the specific business processing requirements of an organization. Implementation must occur before a business can begin to use the R/3 System to process its transactions. Configuration is the process whereby the R/3 System is set up for use by a particular business. This involves specifying the organization structure, selecting the business processes to be implemented, and entering the configuration parameters or settings for the selected business processes. Because this is a complex undertaking, a project team is required to coordinate and conduct the necessary configuration activities. The SAP Solution Manager provides tools that assist in carrying out this configuration following the ASAP methodology. Ultimately, the actual configuration settings are made using the IMG. This procedure often follows a prototyping approach so that end users can confirm the configuration of their R/3 System as the configuration is being performed during the Realization phase of the ASAP Roadmap. This allows deviations between user expectations and the actual configuration to be addressed and enables changes to be made in a more effective and efficient manner. Once the configuration and testing are completed and end users are trained, an organization can begin to use their R/3 System to process the transactions that occur in conducting their business operations. This continues forever on a daily basis, until an R/3 Enterprise System upgrade is available, which will cause additional, incremental configuration and testing to occur throughout the system's life cycle.

Appendix: Quick Check Answers

Chapter 1—Overview

1. False
2. Enterprise Resource Planning (ERP)
3. Business process reengineering (BPR)
4. Event driven
5. True
6. Core
7. Scalability, flexibility, on-going maintenance
8. False
9. Customization

Chapter 2—Navigation and Systems Operation

1. Client, Language
2. Settings
3. Search Help (previously known as matchcodes)
4. List arrow
5. Online Help
6. IDES
7. Status

Chapter 3—Application Modules

1. False
2. Supply chain management
3. Web Application Server (or Basis system)
4. One, consistency
5. Standardized
6. True
7. Business Framework

Chapter 4—Business Processes

1. True
2. Customer Order Management, Manufacturing Planning & Execution, Procurement, and Financial/Managerial Accounting & Reporting

3. False
4. Master
5. Any three of SD, FI, MM, PP, CO
6. Any three of MM, FI, SD, PP, CO, HR
7. Any three of MM, FI, PP, CO, PM
8. FI and CO
9. Customer Order Management, Manufacturing Planning & Execution, and Financial/Managerial Accounting & Reporting
10. Customer delivery

Chapter 5—Web Application Server

1. Presentation, application logic, and data storage
2. True
3. Work
4. Data Dictionary
5. False
6. False
7. OLE

Chapter 6—Internet-Enabled Solutions

1. False
2. Consumer-to-business, business-to-business, intranets
3. Training
4. Mirrors
5. HR
6. True
7. True

Chapter 7—Configuration

1. False
2. SAP Reference Structure, Accelerated SAP (or Solution Manager), ABAP Workbench
3. True
4. SAP Reference Structure
5. Business transaction data, customizing data, business objects
6. True
7. ABAP Workbench
8. False
9. Development system (DEV), quality assurance system (QAS), production system (PRD)
10. Table-driven

Chapter 8—Implementation Framework

1. True
2. ASAP or Accelerated SAP
3. Project Preparation, Business Blueprint, Realization, Final Preparation, Go Live & Support
4. Realization
5. Final Preparation
6. Continuous improvement
7. False
8. Realization

Chapter 9—Organization Structure

1. Uniquely
2. Enterprise Data Model
3. True
4. Company code
5. Financial Accounting view, Controlling view, Sales and Distribution view, Materials Management view
6. Cost center
7. Sales organization
8. Plant
9. Distribution channel
10. False

Chapter 10—Customizing Tools

1. True
2. Accelerator
3. In-scope
4. Cycles
5. Process ID
6. R/3 system
7. True
8. International Standards Organization (ISO)
9. Insert Interval
10. False

Index